CW00539229

WALKING ON BRIDGES

Walks along the packhorse routes and bridges of the Lake District

ROBIN BRAY

HAYLOFT PUBLISHING LTD
KIRKBY STEPHEN

First published by Hayloft 2009

Hayloft Publishing Ltd, South Stainmore,
Kirkby Stephen, Cumbria, CA17 4DJ

tel: 017683 42300
email: books@hayloft.eu
web: www.hayloft.eu

ISBN 1 904524 68 0 (paperback)
ISBN 1 904524 69 9 (hardback)

CAP data for this title are available from the British Library

Designed, printed and bound in the EU

Papers used by Hayloft are natural, recyclable products made from wood grown in
sustainable forest. The manufacturing processes conform to the environmental
regulations of the country of origin.

To my children,

David, Sarah and Joanna

and to the engineers and workmen

who built the bridges

we all take for granted.

LIST OF PLATES

CONTENTS

LIST OF FIGURES

ACKNOWLEDGEMENTS

There are many people I must thank, and books that I must acknowledge. I have done most of the walks by myself but sometimes I was lucky enough to have a companion. Among these were Liz Cunliffe, Pete Bettess, Tess Gallagher, Janet White and, of course, Max the dog.

There are lots of excellent books on the Lake District. The ones that I have used most are mentioned in the bibliography but I must mention four in particular. The first is Diana Whaley's scholarly book on Lake District place names. This is essential for anyone interested in how the mountains, streams and villages in the Lake District acquired their, often intriguing, names and I have shamelessly borrowed from it to add interest to the text. This is only a tasting, however, and you should really try the real thing. Another essential reference book is Ernest Hinchliffe's *Guide to the Packhorse Bridges of England.* It contains the details of scores of bridges, not just in the Lake District, and I have used much of the information gathered by him in my descriptions of individual bridges. Without this book I would not have known of the existence of many of the bridges let alone their histories and statistics.

Another invaluable book is Paul Hindle's *Roads and Tracks of the Lake District.* His research told me where the packhorse trains went from and to and how they worked. As well as packhorse routes, he describes the paths and roads of other ages, from the Romans to the last century. But pride of place must go to Gordon Readyhough and his book of facts on the Lake District. If you want to know anything about anywhere in the National Park then his *The Lake District: The Ultimate Guide* is almost certain to have it. I have used it ceaselessly while writing this book and can only thank him for what must have been a life's work.

Like all researchers these days I am grateful for the 'Net' and in particular 'Wikipedia', an almost unlimited source of information. The other essential has been the collection of the four 1 in 25,000 Explorer Ordnance Survey maps of the National Park. These maps are of course works of precision but they are also works of art and I have spent many hours reading and enjoying them as I would a book. Each walk has been planned and then followed on the appropriate map when I have been writing them up. I have also been very grateful for having them to hand when walking in areas with which I was not previously familiar. The maps reproduced in this book showing where the walks go are from the OS 1 in 50,000 Landranger series digitised by Anquet Maps. Their actual scales in the book vary a little to fit the page size but are approximately 1 in 50,000. I drew the routes and added the place numbers. Susan Devlin helped me with the mapping software and Mike Stafford persuaded my computers to talk to each other and helped with downloading maps. More computer advice was provided by Gerard Carson and Chris Vallis.

I also need to thank Michelle Kelly, the curator, and the voluntary helpers of the Armitt Museum and Library in Ambleside who searched out references for packhorse routes, the staff of Kendal Library who found relevant books, pamphlets and photographs, the curator of the Abbot Hall Art Gallery who searched through dozens of old photographs with me, John Hodgson of the Lake District National Park who provided me with the list of old bridges known to them, Emma Beattie of Capita Symonds who told me about the Callender-Hamilton Bridge at Langwathby, and Georgina Plowright, curator of the English Heritage site at Corbridge, who helped me with Roman bridges. Laurie Rangecroft provided suggestions for the text and introduced me to Professor Bettess. I have also used the maps, digital and otherwise, in the Robinson Library of the University of Newcastle upon Tyne and spent many happy hours working there. Jilly Turner drew the pictures.

I am also very grateful to Professor Peter Bettess, late Professor of Civil Engineering at Durham University. He showed me the bridge at Troutbeck Park, read the technical chapters at the end of the book and corrected many of my misconceptions and errors. I must also thank Dr. Tom Wyatt, late of Imperial College, another engineer, who explained to me the mechanics of the collapse of the Tacoma Narrows Bridge and also read and corrected the technical chapters. John Graham (of Shap) told me about Mardale and its bridges and Stephen White of Carlisle Library provided two images from the Cumbria Image Bank. Malcolm Cundy also read the text.

Finally I must acknowledge the work done by the readers of my manuscript. This is a boring and thankless task but a very necessary one. They pointed out many mistakes but the remaining ones are all mine. Thanks Liz, Tess, Edward, Pete, Tom and Dawn. Thanks again to Dawn Robertson, my publisher, and Edward Hughes, a great teacher, who both believed it would work.

INTRODUCTION

Why bridges, why the Lake District and why me?

The first one is easy. Bridges, or at least good bridges, are a combination of beauty and utility rarely surpassed in human endeavour. There is something immensely pleasing to the eye in an elegant arch, whether it is made of stone, brick, iron or wood, and anyone who has walked across really wild country will know how useful bridges are.

The second is also pretty easy. The English Lake District has an unparalleled collection of old stone arched bridges, all reasonably close together and in countryside which is a delight to walk through. It is also an area where people go to have holidays and therefore have the time to look at things they might otherwise rush past without a second thought.

The "Why me?" is less easy. I first visited the Lake District when I was nine, when my parents took me for a week's holiday to Grasmere, and I fell in love with it. Over the years I have visited the Lake District countless times and have never tired of its hills, lakes and villages. I am not sure when I first noticed the stone bridges but I remember my parents taking me to Grange-in-Borrowdale and pointing out the bridge with its two arches. My parents were not great walkers and tended to drive from one tea shop to the next, but they knew a pretty village when they saw one and Grange was certainly that and the bridge was one of its main attractions.

This book is an attempt to describe some of the stone bridges of the Lake District and how and why they were made and also to say something about bridges in general. The examples of different types of bridge are mainly from the North of England because that is where I live and know best. It is also, perhaps mainly, a walking book. Most of the Lake District bridges were part of the system of packhorse routes that provided commercial transport in the area and I have included some information about them and where they went. As many of these bridges are still there and generally accessible I have listed them and described several walks that go past or over old bridges. Some of these walks are long treks as they follow the packhorse routes from valley to valley and are only for strong walkers. Some do not have any bridges at all but still give an idea of what taking the horses over the passes was like. Others are circular walks that link up different packhorse routes and bring you back to where you started. Again

these can be long but there is no necessity to do the whole walk and turning back is always an option. I have also described some short walks, each
with a bridge, for the less athletic or just those with less time to spare.

In case anyone thinks that I am a terrestrial version of the late Donald
Crowhurst, I have actually walked every inch of the routes that follow
although I have to confess that I have not always done them in the exact
sequences described here. By that I mean I have sometimes divided a long
pass into two sections, usually by doing two circular walks, and then
assembled the information into a single walk over the pass. For example
the passes from Eskdale to Borrowdale are too long to go both ways on a
single day, or at least too long for me. I did one walk going up Ore Gap
and back down Esk Hause and another up Ruddy Gorge and down
Langstrath: the circular walk from Eskdale via Esk Hause, Sty Head and
Burn Moor also covered some of the same ground. I have done most of the
walks more than once but it all takes time and things change and inaccu-
racies creep in. If you find any, let me know and they can be corrected in
future editions, if there are any.

Another problem is that the same bit of a walk may occur in different
contexts. For example a circular walk may contain two half passes which
have been described elsewhere, plus a connecting part which may not have
been. As the description of each walk has to stand by itself, inevitably
there is some repetition and I apologise for this. To reduce this I have made
the descriptions of the (linear) walks over the passes the definitive ones.
They will contain the greatest detail but you will learn most about a walk
by reading about it in all its contexts. The circular walks will have brief
descriptions of the routes already covered but more detail about the connecting parts if they are not covered elsewhere. The descriptions of the
walks are not intended to be completely explicit and, at times, some inter-
pretation may be necessary.

It will always be necessary to have a proper map, such as the Ordnance
Survey 1:25,000, as well as the maps in this book. They are there to give
you an idea of where the walks go and do not purport to be sufficiently
detailed to act as instruments of navigation, mainly for reasons of scale. As
the beginning of a walk is often the most difficult to navigate there is usually more descriptive detail here. Having said all that, I hope this book
encourages you to get out there, enjoy the scenery and do some "Walking
on bridges" and will not be, as one of my friends said, "A bridge too far".

In the technical chapters about bridges (6 and 7) there are one or two
even more technical bits in italics. They are there to provide deeper and
more accurate explanations but can easily be skipped with no loss of con-
tinuity. In fact all the technical chapters can be safely omitted if you just

want to know where the bridges and packhorse routes are but I hope you might become interested enough in bridges to read them at some stage.

Just a word of warning. Although I have letters after my name they are not the right ones for building bridges. I think what I have said about the construction of bridges is correct in engineering terms but this is not a text book and I am not an engineer. Do not be tempted to go out and build your own suspension or cantilever bridge using just the information contained here. If you need to build a bridge, and who does not at some time in his or her life, consult the people who have been appropriately trained. Bridges that fall down are expensive and give other bridges a bad name.

1: SOME THINGS ABOUT BRIDGES

Dr Johnson said that a bridge is "A building raised over water for the convenience of passage" and it is pretty hard to improve on that except, perhaps, to say that a bridge is not always over water. A bridge is a structure to allow passage from one piece of land to another where there is some discontinuity or obstacle on the land's surface. In other words it gets you from one side to the other. These days bridges can be over roads, usually motorways, or railways or canals but generally they are still for getting over

rivers, particularly in wild country. A river, particularly a deep or rapidly-flowing one, is a major obstacle to progress. Not only is it difficult to cross, it is potentially dangerous. Indeed in mountainous countryside fast-moving streams and rivers are among the most dangerous parts of any journey and crossing them is best avoided. They are equally difficult and dangerous for animals and wheeled vehicles so it is easy to see why considerable effort has gone

Plate 1: Stepping stones over the River Rothay near Rydal

into making river crossings easier and safer.

Small streams can be jumped in one or several stages. As the streams become wider and deeper this quickly becomes hazardous and slippery stones have caused many broken bones and even drownings. It may well be safer, although colder and wetter, to wade across the river bed rather than risk a fall. The approved method is to remove one's socks and walk across wearing boots. Although getting your boots soaked is psychologically damaging, they provide grip and protection for the feet and eventually they dry out. It needs remarkably little depth of rapidly flowing water for a person to lose his or her footing and be swept down river, and mountaincraft books contain many pages of advice about crossing rivers. The simplest involves wading the river using a stick for support or huddling in a group shaped to present the least resistance to the river's downstream thrust. The more complicated methods use ropes secured on each bank after the first person has made the crossing using an anchor point and a pendulum traverse.

The simplest means of improving short and shallow crossings is to place flat stones as stepping stones, at convenient intervals across the stream. Large, flat-topped stones make it easier for people to retain their balance but animals and vehicles do not find them much help. Also the water level in most streams varies considerably and the stepping stones may become submerged or slippery. A ford is a safer prospect for animals and vehicles. A ford is a place where the river has been allowed to spread out, so that depth of water has been converted to width to make it easier to cross. It also allows the banks to be lower, or non existent, to make entry and exit easier. Generally fords are only possible in fairly flat country and even then they become hazardous when the river is in spate. A bridge is an enormous improvement.

The two materials that were most important for building the bridges in the Lake District were wood and stone. The early bridges were usually made from wood and have not survived, presumably because they rotted, and were replaced by the stone bridges that we see today. Stone, usually slate, was available locally and is still quarried there. It is easily worked because it can be split along its 'grain' and can be used in smallish slabs which can be transported and handled without too much difficulty. Wood, of course, is even easier to work.

Wood and stone have quite different properties and have to be used in different ways. This will be considered in greater detail in the last two chapters but for now it is sufficient to say that wood is reasonably strong when it is pulled apart (i.e. in tension) and also when it is squashed (i.e. in compression) whereas stone is weak in tension but strong in compression.

Wood is therefore a more versatile building material that can be used to make almost any structure, but for longevity it needs to be protected from fire and water. To be safe, stone has to be kept in compression. This means that wooden bridges and stone bridges have different designs.

The simplest type of bridge is a tree trunk stretching from one bank to the other, in engineering terms a beam. Even the word 'beam' means tree in Old English, hence hornbeam and whitebeam. Trees of an appropriate size do not always grow conveniently on the river bank, but if they do chopping them down and encouraging them to fall across the river is an easy way of building a bridge. The span of such a bridge is limited by the height and girth of available trees and by the difficulty of transporting the tree to the site, should that be necessary. It is a small step to flatten the top of the tree trunk and lay several side by side to make a bridge that is less of a balancing act to cross. Covering the top with branches placed cross-wise and filling the gaps with compacted earth makes an even better surface. As technology improved, the ability to make sawn planks became more common and bridge building became easier and more adaptable.

Wood is an almost ideal material for a simple beam. In other words it is capable of withstanding the compression and tension that will be produced within it by its own weight and the loads that it carries. Hence most wooden bridges are beams of one sort or another. They are easy to build

Plate 2: A modern wooden beam bridge with stone piers at White Moss Common, near Rydal.

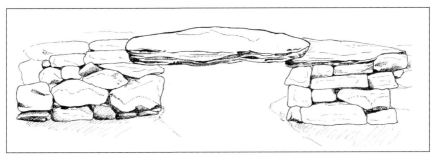

Fig. 1: A stone beam (clapper) bridge

although longer bridges may need to be supported at intervals by piers standing in the water. Their only real disadvantage is that they rot and have to be replaced at intervals.

Stone, on the other hand, is not a suitable material for making beams and will tend to crack underneath where it is exposed to tension. There are stone beam bridges in the Lake District and elsewhere, but compared with wooden beams they have short spans. These are the clapper or clam bridges and some will be described later. Because of their limitations even quite small streams have to be bridged with multiple spans.

The secret to using stone safely is to keep it firmly in compression. This is easy in buildings, you just put one stone on top of another, but to bridge a gap an arch is needed. An arch is a set of stones (or something similar) called voussoirs, each slightly wedge-shaped, forming all or part of a semicircle (or something similar). The weight of the arch, and any load on it, pushes the stones together and the greater the load the greater the compression. As long as this compression is not so great that the stone shatters, and its abutments stay sound, the arch will remain intact. The individual stones are kept in place by a combination of the compression generated by the arch, the friction between the stones and any masonry above the arch pressing down onto it.

The arch is an ancient structure, perhaps dating back as far as 6,000 years. There are remains of brick arches in Egypt and Mesopotamia from about 3,600 BC forming parts of buildings. The Chinese seem to have been the first to have used arches to bridge small streams around 2,500 BC. The arch appears to have developed separately from corbelling (the bridging of a gap by placing each successive stone a little further out until they meet in the middle) which works in quite a different way. The Romans made extensive use of arches in buildings and bridges. Many Roman arched bridges have survived to this day, although, sadly, none in Britain. Roman arches were semicircular but this is not necessary to make a bridge safe. As long as the stones make some sort of arch it will usually be secure, but

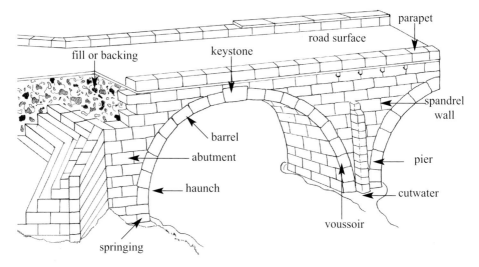

Fig. 2: A stone arch bridge with its parts named.

the flatter the arch, the greater the sideways thrust against the abutments and the shorter the distance it has to sink before it becomes flat and fails. Even a semicircular arch has some sideways thrust and will not stand up without support from its abutments.

Most Roman bridges in Britain were made from wood and have not survived. The more important ones had stone piers and a few, such as those at Chesters and Corbridge in Northumberland, had stone arches as well. (The remains of their abutments and ramps can be easily viewed from public pathways on the opposite sides of the river from their respective forts. Both paths start from nearby beautiful stone arched bridges; an added bonus.) After the Romans left, the building of stone arched bridges lapsed but revived in the twelfth century under the patronage of the church. As well as building semicircular arches, where the centre of the circle is at the level of the base, segmental arches began to be used. A segmental arch is one in which the arch forms less than half of the circumference of a circle and the centre of the circle is below the base of the arch. It is therefore flatter and more economical to build and easier to cross as its rise is less. Pointed arches have two centres below the base; some have even more. Other designs are based on the ellipse. Most stone bridges, including those in the Lake District, have segmental arches.

The business bit of an arched bridge, the arch itself, is generally referred to as the barrel. This is not necessarily what it seems on the outside as larger stones may have been used for the visible work for aesthetic reasons but in the Lake District bridges the barrel is usually clearly visible.

The central, or key stone, has no particular structural importance over the other voussoirs. Above the arch was placed fill, usually just rubble or the material excavated during the building work. The fill was held in place by the side walls (spandrel walls) and may have a waterproof covering. All this helps a little to strengthen the bridge, in the sense that fill above the arch stops the voussoirs popping out under load, but it also increases the dead load (the weight of the bridge itself).

On occasion the weight of the backing (the fill on either side of the arch) has even pushed the crown of the arch upwards to the point of failure, as it did in the bridge at Pontypridd in about 1755. One of the reasons for passages being constructed through the backings, as seen in some bridges, is to reduce the mass of the material here and so reduce the load on the haunches of the bridge. Any mortar between adjacent arch stones serves to spread the compressive load more evenly; it has little or no tensile strength. The original Lake District bridges just consisted of a slate or stone arch with no fill or walls, which was an efficient and economical construction, but many have been altered over the years. The early bridges were built without mortar which is sometimes a way of telling which half of a widened bridge is the older.

Just like beam bridges there is a limit to the size of a masonry span, at least if the arch is not to reach too great a height and the bridge is not to collapse under its own weight. An arch can be significantly longer than a simple wooden beam bridge but for practical purposes a wide river has to be crossed with several arches. Unless there are convenient islands the piers between the arches have to be built in the river and down to material strong enough to support their weight and that of half the arch on each side. Roman multi-arch bridges had massive supporting piers, with widths a quarter to one third of the adjacent arch spans, which were usually substantial enough to allow one arch to collapse without the rest falling as well. Although this was a way of preventing passage in times of war without having to rebuild the whole bridge later it was also a way of constructing

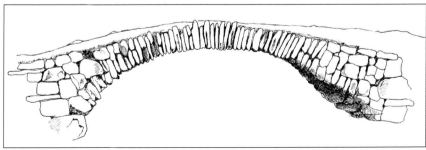

Fig. 3: A typical Lake District packhorse bridge.

a multi-arch bridge or viaduct one arch at a time. In similar fashion some modern viaducts, such as the magnificent one at Ribblehead, have one or more thicker piers, enabling the building work to have started from several places at the same time. It is also a safety measure to reduce the chance of progressive failure. Many piers have rounded or pointed upstream extensions, called cutwaters, to reduce the thrust on the piers. In older, narrow, bridges, the piers may extend upwards to provide refuges for pedestrians. There are one or two stone multi-arch bridges in the Lake District, such as the one at Grange-in-Borrowdale (NY 254174) and Pelter Bridge, by the road between Ambleside and Rydal (NY 366059).

An arch may fail because the abutments move apart under the load from the arch, or apart or sideways in an earthquake. Significant earthquakes are unusual in the Lake District and most of the abutments are founded on solid lumps of rock and are unlikely to move much. Only very rarely does an arch fail because its constituent stones crumble from an excessive load. Much more likely is that the lateral force of a river in spate pushes the bridge downstream and it collapses. Bridges with piers in the river are obviously more vulnerable to this but even single arches are not immune. Some bridge designs make provision for abnormally high flows by having passages above the piers and between the arches or by having redundant arches at the sides which come into use at times of spate as well as lightening the structure. These features are not seen in the Lake District packhorse bridges although they may be built with an arch size that can accommodate abnormally large flows.

There are several disadvantages to building arches. The stone may have to be transported some distance and stone is heavy. It is also less easy to work than wood and building the bridge is more complicated and therefore more expensive. The arch needs to be supported from below during its

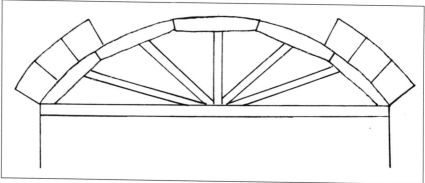

Fig. 4:. A stone arch being constructed with wooden centring in place

construction and is only stable once the arch is complete. The support is provided by wooden 'false work' or centring, usually a rough wooden arch that bridges the gap and supports the individual stones until the stone arch is finished. The stones are put into place in roughly equal numbers on each side of the false work and when the keystone is placed in the centre the arch becomes stable. Leonardo da Vinci said that at this moment, "Two weaknesses become a strength." The false work can now be removed and the arch 'settles'.

Another disadvantage is that the roadway has to rise over the arch (a 'humpbacked' bridge) which makes life difficult for heavily-laden animals and vehicles. The way around this is either to build a slowly-rising ramp up to the bridge, which is expensive and time consuming and you still have the same height gain, or to start the arch lower down on the banks of the river so that the top of the arch is at the level of the river banks. As railway engines do not like humpbacked bridges at all this was usually the solution for railway arches. The disadvantage here is that there may not be much of a river bank, which is often the case in the Lake District, and the arch may be more immersed in the river and therefore more vulnerable to a sideways push.

In spite of these disadvantages, stone arched bridges are often the best and most durable choice. There is a wonderful inscription on a triumphal arch over the Puente Trajan crossing the river Tagus in Spain placed there by its builder, Julius Lacer, in AD 104. In translation it reads, "I have built a bridge that shall remain forever." Apart from one arch having to be rebuilt after being blown up in 1809 to halt the French army, Lacer's promise has held true.

Not the least reason to build a stone arched bridge is that they are, or at least can be, things of grace and beauty, and we need more of those in our lives.

2: THE LAKE DISTRICT STONE BRIDGES

Plate 3: Stockley Bridge in 1814 (courtesy of Carlisle Library).

The old Lake District stone-arch bridges that we see today were mainly built over a period of about 100 years starting around 1660 and some, such as Sadgill (1717) and Winster (1729), can be dated quite accurately. Ogilby's map of 1670 shows stone bridges at Grasmere and Dunmail Raise. Many were built to replace existing wooden bridges, presumably in poor repair, some of which would have had stone piers, others wooden posts. After about 1760, when the turnpike roads were being built, wider and stronger bridges were needed to cope with the carriages. The ones that we shall consider most are the arched bridges but the stone-beam clapper bridges also played a part and some will have pre-dated the arched bridges. The word clapper comes from the Old English *cleaca* meaning "bridging the stepping stones" and some have multiple, simple piers that look just like stepping stones.

For reasons that have already been considered the single-span clapper bridges can only cross small streams. Although functional they lack the grace of an arch and perhaps for that reason they have been less studied but they still "get you from one side to the other." The arched bridges were mainly built to serve the wool trade which needed packhorses for transport. Heavily laden packhorse trains would have found fording rivers more hazardous than unladen sheep or cattle would have done and this provided the necessary economic stimulus. Packhorse routes criss-cross the Lake District and many of the surviving bridges are found on them. A puzzling few seem off such routes and may have had other purposes, such as just a way between fields or to a mill or mine, but are still called packhorse bridges.

The definition of a packhorse bridge is not absolute. To be called such it helps if they are known to be of the period and are less than about two metres wide as the horses walked in a single file. Also they were built without parapets so as not to catch on the panniers. Even better is if they lie on a known packhorse route. No doubt I have omitted some that deserve to be included in the list that follows and I might even have included some that should not have been. If so, I apologise, but the histories of individual bridges are often sketchy with little having been written down. With one or two exceptions, not much is known about the organisation and financing of their building. In an earlier period the monasteries controlled the wool trade and probably built the bridges but the dissolution of the monasteries was complete by 1540 and most packhorse bridges, at least in the Lake District, were built more recently.

The bridges are made of slate or other stone, depending on what was available locally. Slate cleaves (or rives) to form parallel surfaces and not the wedge shapes sought by arch builders. In this case the arch is made by using mortar or smaller pieces of slate, to pad out the greater circumference. Other types of stone could be selected for their wedge shapes. Some now have side walls and even railings for safety reasons, such as the Walna Scar bridge near Coniston, but many remain as they were. They are of rustic construction and as Hinchliffe says, "look as though a dry stone waller had built them whilst seeking a change from his normal work." This is not to say that building skills are redundant. With commendable originality Magnus Linklater, a columnist for *The Times*, commissioned a dry stone bridge to celebrate his 35 years of marriage but when the false work was removed the first version collapsed into the river below.

Most of the bridges are accessible to the walker and some are close to towns and villages. The best listing of them is found in Ernest Hinchliffe's excellent book and much of what follows, including the grid references, is taken from that. All the measurements are approximate. Hinchliffe grades the bridges into three groups. Those in group one are the most authentic

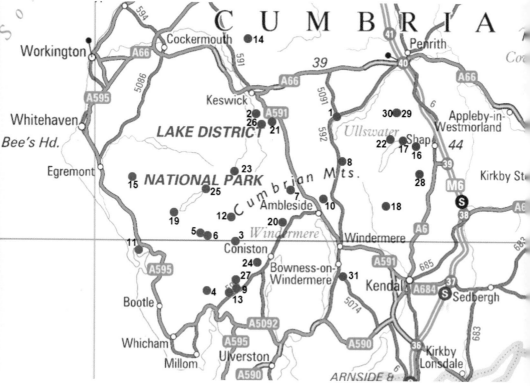

Map 1: The Lake District, showing the packhorse bridges mentioned in the text.
© *Crown Copyright and/or database right. All rights reserved. Licence number 100048757.*

1) Aira Beck
2) Ashness
3) Birks
4) Bleabeck
5) Boot
6) Doctor
7) Far Easedale
8) Hartsop
9) (near) Hawk Bridge
10) High Sweden
11) Holme
12) Lingcove
13) Lind End
14) Mirkholme
15) Monks
16) Parish Crag

17) Park
18) Sadgill
19) Scale
20) Slater
21) Smaithwaite
22) Stanegarth
23) Stockley
24) Walna Scar
25) Wasdale Head
26) Watendlath
27) Water Yeat
28) Wet Sleddale
29) Widewath 1
30) Widewath 2
31) Winster

(less than two metres wide, built before 1800 and with known packhorse associations). Group two fail in one respect and group three fail in more but can be just as delightful. For the purposes of this book I shall stick to those within the National Park. What follows is an alphabetical list with short descriptions of the bridges and how to find them. The names are those used on the OS maps. It is possible to walk, or in some cases even drive, just to see the bridge but for a more authentic experience why not do a walk over the old packhorse route (if there is one) and use the bridge for its original purpose.

Plate 4: Aira Beck Bridge

1) *Aira Beck* (Gp 2) NY401201

Aira Force is a noted beauty spot near to the north bank of Ullswater, but few people pause to look at the nearby bridge a short distance downstream of the waterfall and adjacent to the east side of the National Trust car park, although on private land. It is in good repair but is somewhat overgrown with moss and ivy. It is about three metres wide with a span of four metres. There are no parapets. It is thought to be on a trackway from a plantation to the north and a mill just west of Lyulph's Tower. There are certainly the remains of a mill race on the west bank which starts upstream of the bridge and travels through a buried pottery pipe about half a metre in diameter to a masonry outlet downstream of the bridge. Lyulph's tower was built in the late eighteenth century by Charles Howard of Greystoke, probably on a more ancient site. The name comes from Ligulf, said to be an ancestor of the Greystokes.

2) *Ashness Bridge* (Gp 3) NY270196

This must be one of the most-photographed bridges in the Lake District. Not because of its virtues as a bridge but because of where it is. It has a magnificent backdrop with Skiddaw in the distance. It carries the tarmac road from Watendlath to the Borrowdale Valley and it, or more likely a predecessor, may have eased the passage of packhorses travelling down towards Keswick although the traffic, in those days at least, cannot have been very heavy. Ashness means the headland where ash trees grow.

3) *Birks Bridge* (Gp 2) SD234993

Birks refers to birches. This is another bridge that has been much photographed, partly because it is easy of access with a nearby car park but also because of its setting in the lovely Duddon Valley. It is unusual in having drainage pipes set at intervals at road level through the parapet wall. Why this bridge and not others should have such drains is obscure as it is unlikely that rain water would collect to any extent on an arch. Perhaps it was just an experiment that was found to be an unnecessary complication and was therefore not repeated. Its span is about three and a half metres and its width almost two.

Plate 5: Birks Bridge.

4) *Bleabeck Bridge* (Gp 3) SD188919

This is a small bridge that is not as easy to reach as the two mentioned above. It has parapets and has been widened from about two metres to more than three with an obvious join underneath, the older part is upstream. Its span is a little more than three and a half metres. It crosses Blea (dark) Beck before it goes down to join the River Duddon but does not appear to be on a known packhorse route. Perhaps it was just on a farm path between fields or provided an easier way down to the valley for the denizens of the now-ruined Frith Hall. The bridge can be visited by walking along the path that arises on the left of the road that comes up from Ulpha in Dunnerdale.

5) *Boot* (Gp 2) NY177012

This lovely bridge is in the centre of Boot just next to the old water mill. It has parapets, and is almost two metres wide with a span of more than eight metres. The mill is now a museum and is well worth a visit to see working medieval technology. Not to be missed, and relevant to this book, it displays a padded wooden pack-saddle used to carry sacks of corn. The display notes that there was once a gang of twenty packhorses that passed through Boot each week on the way to Ambleside over Hardknott and Wrynose Passes. The bridge crosses Whillan Beck on the route to and from Wasdale Head via Burn Moor. This was an old corpse road (see later, Burn Moor and Mardale Corpse Road) as well as a packhorse route. There were also several iron ore mines around here, the largest and the last to close, in 1917, was at Nab Gill. No doubt they provided some trade for the route as well. It is easy to reach the bridge although parking nearby is difficult. It might be as well to have a cup of tea at the nearby pub and park there or walk from the car park at the Eskdale end of the narrow gauge railway from Ravenglass at Dalegarth. The name Boot has nothing to do with footwear and may come from the Middle English for a bend, which the valley does here.

6) *Doctor (Eskdale) Bridge* (Gp 2) NY189008

This bridge is not far from Boot and can be visited at the same time as the bridge there. Either walk along the road towards Hardknott Pass or park on the quiet road nearby. The bridge crosses the Esk and was at the junction of the route from Ravenglass to Ambleside which went along the south side of the Esk and a longer route that came from Whitehaven via Skalderskew and Mitredale. The former can still be walked although on a road where it goes over the passes but the latter is less obvious as it gets further from Eskdale. The bridge was widened in 1737 by a local doctor called Edward Tyson who lived at Penny Hill, just down the road, so that he could cross in his pony and trap. The original arch is still visible from below with the older part upstream. It has parapets, a span of about eleven metres and a width of about three and a half. The original width was about a metre and a half.

7) *Far Easedale (Willie Goodwaller)* (Gp 2) NY322088

It is difficult to get a close look at this bridge as it is on private farmland but the determined can always ask the farmer, which is what I did. You can see it in the distance from a short stretch of the path up to Easedale Tarn (see Short Walks 2, Far Easedale from Grasmere, page 114). There are no parapets. The span is about three metres and the width a little greater at about three and a half metres. It is between two fields, is fairly crude and is a replacement for the original. It is said that the first bridge was built without mortar over Willie's back as he bent over in the stream. If true, he must have had a strong back and a pretty wide one but it does make the point that as long as something holds the two incomplete arches up, when the arch is complete it does not matter what the something was as long as it was strong enough, roughly the right shape and can be removed easily.

The first bridge was washed away, illustrating one of the weaknesses of masonry bridges, and the replacement was said to have been built by Willie's brother. Whether Willie played any part in the second construction is unrecorded. The bridge does not seem to be on any packhorse route and may just have been a farm bridge. Hinchliffe thinks there may have been an even older bridge at this spot which served a fulling mill in Far Easedale. Fulling was a process in which cloth was made 'fuller' or more dense by being passed between water-powered rollers. At one time the area now called Cumbria was said to posses more than 500 such mills.

8) *Hartsop* (Gp 2) NY410129

Hartsop is a delightful village and well worth a visit even if it didn't have a bridge. Note the spinning galleries as you walk through the village. The bridge is over Pasture Beck, just after the car park on the far side of the village. It may have been on the route from Patterdale to Ambleside via Kirkstone Pass or, less probably, Scandale Pass. Either route seems to involve a bit of a detour. Perhaps it was something to do with the mines just up the valley. The bridge itself has been widened to just over three metres and has iron railings although there is no parapet. The span is about four and a half metres. Hartsop means place of the stag or hart and there are still deer around here. It is also from 'hop' which referred to a rounded or blind valley.

9) (near) *Hawk Bridge* (Gp 3) SD236918

This bridge is near to, but distinct from, the Hawk Bridge on the OS map. The latter is a road bridge on the minor road coming up from Broughton Mills. It is not easy to see the packhorse bridge as it is in some woodland about 100 metres downstream of the official Hawk Bridge. There is no path from the road but it is possible, with some care, to reach it by walking along the right bank of the river. There are some ruined farm buildings nearby and it is likely that the bridge served them. The whole area is overgrown and the bridge looks forlorn and neglected. Like so many others the bridge has been widened; the downstream half has been built without mortar and so is probably the older part. On the apex of the arch the barrel stones are exposed. The span is about five and a half metres and the width two and a half.

10) *High Sweden Bridge* (Gp 1) NY379068

This is a well-known bridge as it is at the start of the Fairfield Horseshoe, at least if you go round it the way Wainwright recommends. It is not on the obvious route from Ambleside to Scandale Pass and so must have had another purpose such as linking fields or perhaps using the other way up from Ambleside to Scandale via Low Sweden Bridge, or more likely a predecessor. It consists of an arch of stones with no coverings or parapets and has remained at its original width of about 1.7 metres. The span is about 4.3 metres. The bridge is flattened at the apex but seems perfectly stable. In Wainwright's first book, *The Eastern Fells*, there is a drawing of the bridge in the description of the walk up Low Pike in which it does not appear to be flattened. This book was published in 1955 and no doubt the drawing was made some time before, suggesting that the settling is relatively recent. It is easy to find by walking up the road from Ambleside as described under Scandale Pass and in the short walks section. The name sweden is nothing to do with the country but is from *swidden* or an area of moorland cleared by burning.

11) *Holme (Drigg) Bridge* (Gp 1) SD076987

Drigg means a place of dragging, presumably of boats across a shore and holme was a piece of land surrounded by streams. Holme Bridge is on the old packhorse road from Ravenglass to Drigg and the north. It crosses the River Irt, which is the outflow from Wast Water, less than a mile south east of Drigg. The bridge is now on the Cumbria Coastal Way and has the unusual honour of being referred to as a packhorse bridge on the OS map. I assume this title is given only to the best and most genuine. It is made of red sandstone, is about 1.8 metres wide and has a high segmental arch of

Plate 6: Holme Bridge.

about eleven and a half metres span with a cobbled footway and parapets capped with mortar. According to the County Index it was probably built in the eighteenth century.

It can be reached by a short walk from the A595 as it goes past Carleton Hall. There is limited parking on the side road to Saltcoats. Go down the farm track beside 'Coach House' to reach a field. Then turn left and follow the track at the edge of the field. Turn right at the corner of the field and eventually go over a stile and across another field heading for a dip in the land where the trees start. A path then leads down to the river. Turn left at the river and the bridge is about 50 metres further on.

12) *Lingcove Bridge* (Gp 1) NY228038

Lingcove Bridge, called Throstlegarth by Hinchliffe and Yew Bank by the Lake District National Park, crosses Lingcove Beck where it joins the River Esk. It has no parapets worth talking about and is really just an arch and is said to have been repaired some time around 1928. Its span is about six and a half metres and its width 1.2 metres. It is on the route from Eskdale to Borrowdale via Esk Hause, perhaps used by the monks of Furness Abbey. The route over Ore Gap passes to the side. It can be reached by walking about three kilometres along the Esk Valley from the road between Eskdale and Ambleside just before it starts to go up to Hardknott Pass (see the short walks section). There is space for parking there. Go on the path to the left of Brotherikeld Farm and close to the river.

Hardknott means a hard or rugged peak. Readyhough says that Hardknott's original name was Wainscarth meaning the "gap through which a wagon could go." Throstlegarth means a thrush enclosure and lingcove a "cove by the torrents" or a "heathery cove."

13) *Lind End Bridge* (Gp 2) SD230913

Lind End Bridge is conveniently close to Hawk Bridge and even closer to Broughton Mills should you be planning to visit both bridges on the same trip. Go up the valley road about half a mile from Broughton Mills and turn left onto a short footpath at Lind End and descend to the river. The footpath continues through the woods up the far side of the valley. The bridge crosses the River Lickle and Hinchliffe thinks it was probably built for packhorses carrying charcoal produced in the woods above the river. There are no parapets, its span is about four and a half metres and the bridge may have been widened to its present two and a half metres.

14) *Mirkholme Bridge* (Gp 3) NY254326

This bridge crosses Halls Beck near to Mirkholme Farm. It is wider than a typical packhorse bridge but there is no sign of a join underneath to indicate a later widening. The stones are mortared but the arch appears typical. There are no stone parapets but ugly steel crash barriers have been added. It does not appear to be on any packhorse route and was probably a farm bridge. To visit it go from Bassenthwaite (village) along secondary roads to Peter House Farm (see Skiddaw). About half a kilometre further on take a farm road on the right which crosses the fields to Mirkholme Farm. The bridge, which is on private land, is through the farm yard and about 100 metres down a rough track.

15) *Monks Bridge* (Gp 1) NY063102

There are various names attached to this bridge including High Wath Bridge, Mattie Benn's Bridge, Hannah Benn's Brig and Roman Bridge. The OS map prefers Monks (should it not be Monk's or even Monks'?) The monks probably came from Calder Abbey, one of the rich and powerful Cistercian monasteries, about five kilometres downstream of the bridge. The ruins can still be seen on the north side of the River Calder. The name may have come from an earlier, and probably wooden, bridge as the existing bridge is thought to be seventeenth or eighteenth century.

To view the bridge, walk down from the junction of minor roads at Friar's Well (NY055101); more monastery associations. There is space for parking here. The clear path keeps to the left of Friar's Gill as it descends to the River Calder. Cross the river on a wooden footbridge, turn left and

Plate 7: Monks Bridge.

walk beside the river for two or three minutes. Monks Bridge crosses a small gorge with a deep pool downstream. It is built of red sandstone, without parapets but with alternate stones projecting horizontally on each side along the top of the arch. The bridge itself is a curious shape with a pointed asymmetrical arch. The pathway is about a metre wide and the span about eight metres. There is some mortaring and small pieces of slate have been inserted between the arch stones.

The bridge almost seems to be on the route from Eskdale to Whitehaven but is slightly to the north. There was also an old drove road that went from Gosforth to Cockermouth but which again just seems to have missed this bridge. Hinchliffe thinks it may have been used for transporting iron ore for smelting as there was once a bloomery at Thornholme about a kilometre or so downstream.

16) *Parish Crag Bridge* (Rosgill) (Gp 1) NY536159

Walkers on the Coast to Coast route pass over this bridge which is in a delightful setting over a sharp bend in Swindale Beck. It is easily reached by a short walk from the road between Rosgill and Bampton. Hinchliffe calls it Rosgill. The ruins of Shap Abbey are nearby. There is a route that goes between Shap and Bampton via the Abbey that passes over the bridge. The Bampton end is now a road. The bridge has a wide span (about eight metres, according to Hinchliffe), parapets and what looks like the original road surface which is about a metre wide.

17) *Park Bridge* (Gp 2) NY515161

The OS map calls this Park Bridge but Hinchliffe prefers Burnbanks. It crosses Haweswater Beck, the outflow from Haweswater. It is reached by a short path across a field from Naddle Gate on the road to Haweswater from Bampton. There are no parapets but wooden railings have been added. It has a span of over eight metres and a width of almost two metres. Hinchliffe wonders if it was on an old route between Bampton Common and Shap, or perhaps connecting the now-submerged road from Mardale Green that led alongside the western side of Haweswater. The dam that did the submerging is not far away upstream. The workers who built the dam were housed in prefabricated bungalows at nearby Burnbanks.

18) *Sadgill* (Gp 2) NY483057

Longsleddale valley is aptly named. It stretches about ten kilometres in a north-westerly direction from the boundary of the National Park at Garnett Bridge, itself about six kilometres north of Kendal, to Gatescarth Pass. Packhorse routes passed along the valley and over Stile End to Kentmere. Gatescarth led to Mardale, Wet Sleddale, Swindale and ultimately to Shap and Penrith. At Sadgill, where the drovers' road from Kentmere joins, the River Sprint is a significant obstacle and in 1717 a successful petition to build a bridge was got up. It has since been widened and the join can be seen underneath. It has a span of about nine metres and a width of almost three. At some stage parapets have been added. The bridge must be of great use to the farm just on the Kentmere side. It can be reached by car coming up the valley and there is ample parking alongside the road. Much nicer though is to include it in a walk along one or more of the old routes.

19) *Scale Bridge* (Gp 2) NY133045

There are three Scale Bridges in Readyhough's book but this is the one over Cinderdale Beck. A dale is a narrow valley and the cinder part refers to the slag heaps produced by the local bloomeries. The bridge is on a track from Nether Wasdale to Scale and then onto Copeland Forest. In medieval times this was an extensive forest used for hunting but it is now treeless, a fate no doubt hastened by the need for charcoal for the iron smelters. You can see the bridge by walking along a track that leaves the road east of Nether Wasdale at Cinderbeck Bridge. Parking may be easier at Nether Wasdale in which case there is a short walk down the road to Cinderbeck Bridge.

The track is sign-posted to Gill and Buckbarrow and goes alongside fields, through Mill Place and then gently uphill. Take the right fork and walk with the wall to your right along a clear path for about half a kilometre. The path then forks to the right, through a gap in the wall by a signpost to Buckbarrow. The bridge is just across the field (see Short Walk 6, page 120). The bridge has parapets, the upstream one continuing as a wall. The surface is stoney and is about three metres wide with a span of about seven metres.

20) *Slater Bridge* (Gp 1) NY312030

As its name suggests this bridge was probably made for the convenience of local slate quarriers who needed to cross the River Brathay. Several dis-used quarries can be found on both sides of the Little Langdale valley but presumably those on the south side were the relevant ones. The bridge is easy to reach from the road going along the floor of Little Langdale although it means crossing a few fields. The road is narrow and parking is limited. The arched bridge is reached by crossing a two-span clapper bridge. It does not have parapets but has an iron railing. The span of the arch is about one and a half metres and the width a little over a metre. The two bridges have great charm and the setting is delightful. It is much pho-tographed and in my view, deservedly so. Hinchliffe calls it Stang End.

Plate 8: Slater Bridge.

21) *Smaithwaite* (Gp 2) NY314194

Thirlmere is a lake that has been turned into a reservoir by Manchester Corporation. For that reason, like Haweswater, it has a barren fringe where the water level rises and falls much more than it does on a natural lake. Smaithwaite Bridge is about half a mile downstream of the dam that made Thirlmere what it is today. It has a span of about four and a half metres and

Plate 9: Smaithwaite Bridge.

a width of about three. The bridge is on the route between Grasmere and Keswick via Dunmail Raise, now a busy road, and from Glenridding over Sticks Pass. It is easily accessed by turning off the main Keswick to Grasmere road just beyond the north end of Thirlmere and travelling a short distance down the minor road that ultimately goes down the west side of the reservoir. It is close to Bridge End Farm. The bridge itself is marooned in the centre of St John's Beck but is connected by wooden bridges at each end. Presumably the stream was somewhat smaller when the original bridge was built.

22) *Stanegarth* (Gp 2) NY496178

This is not mentioned by Hinchliffe but appears to be a genuine packhorse bridge and is listed as an ancient monument. It is probably seventeenth century. The arch is about two metres wide, with a span of four and a half metres and rises four and a half metres at the apex. It has no parapets and is almost a pure, and rather flat, arch. The surface looks recently restored. It has dry stone wing walls about 1.2 metres high at each corner support. The bridge crosses Cawdale Beck just before it reaches the hamlet of Stanegarth and is about 150 metres downstream of an excellent clapper bridge (see below, Cawdale). It does not appear to be near any known packhorse route which, in my view, makes it a group 2. It can be viewed by driving up the road from Bampton to Moorahill Farm and walking south east across some rough ground for about half a kilometre. It is marked as a foot bridge on the OS map.

Plate 10: Stanegarth Bridge.

23) *Stockley Bridge* (Gp 2) NY235109

This bridge was rebuilt after being partially demolished by Grains Gill during the floods in the Borrowdale Valley in 1966. It is on the packhorse route from Borrowdale to Wasdale via Sty Head Pass and on the less-used path to Eskdale via Esk Hause. It has parapets which are castellated. The span is about four and a half metres and its width almost two metres. It is reached by walking along the path from Seathwaite Farm where there is ample parking and even refreshments. Stockley comes from stocks or stakes and the 'ley' part is from the Old English *leah* meaning woodland clearing or meadow.

24) *Walna Scar* (Gp 2) SD271965

The Walna Scar road goes from Coniston to the Duddon Valley and a fair length of it has to be walked to see the bridge. Although a little marred by hand rails it is in a fine setting and on an important route. The arch has small parapets and has been widened at some stage, the downstream, and larger, part being the older. It appears to be marked on Brasiers Map of 1745 where it is referred to as the 'New Bridge'. Its span is about three and a half metres and its width almost two and a half metres.

Starting from Coniston, leave the centre and head north west on a secondary road leading to the old mines. Turn left at some woodland, along a road sign-posted 'Walna Scar Coniston Old Man', and climb up the steep road with trees on the left. The road reaches open fields and then wilder land as it skirts the side of Coniston Old Man. The bridge crosses Torver Beck before the path climbs to go over Walna Scar itself. It is about three kilometres from Coniston where there is ample parking.

25) *Wasdale Head* (Gp 2) NY187088

This is another classic packhorse bridge in a wonderful setting. It is behind the Wasdale Head Hotel, which is just as much a classic in its own way, and crosses Mosedale Beck. Currently it does not seem to be on any pack-horse route but the details of routes change and it may be that the path down from the Black Sail Pass originally came down the other side of Mosedale beck. More likely, Hinchliffe thinks, is that it was on the route from Borrowdale over Sty Head and onwards along the north side of Wast Water. It might just have been a farm bridge though. The bridge is an arch with no parapets. Its span is over eight metres and its width 1.2 metres.

26) *Watendlath* (Gp 1) NY275162

Another famous and much-photographed bridge. It crosses the outlet from Watendlath Tarn next to the delightful hamlet of Watendlath. The bridge has parapets which were added some time between 1902 and 1907 and has a span of almost seven metres and a width of a little over one metre. There is a stone inscribed 'H.R.H. CHARLES 22-5-95' on the Rosthwaite end of the roadway commemorating Prince Charles' visit after the bridge had been restored. It is on the packhorse route from Rosthwaite in Borrowdale to Wythburn at the southern end of Thirlmere which was used for carrying wool. It is easily reached by coming up the road from Borrowdale which provides an opportunity to view Ashness Bridge on the way. A more ener-getic alternative is by a pleasant walk from Rosthwaite.

27) *Water Yeat Bridge* (Gp 2) SD239930

Just up the road from Hawk Bridge and its nearby packhorse bridge is Water Yeat Bridge over the River Lickle. This seems to be a fertile area for packhorse bridges as Lind End is also close by. An easy walk of about three kilometres covers all three although a little off-road walking is needed near Hawk Bridge. The bridge carries the minor road from Broughton Mills which loops round connecting three farms originally founded by Furness Abbey. There appears to be a route that goes from Ravenglass on the coast to Coniston via Waberthwaite Fell, Ulpha in Dunnerdale, and Torver, although this is not shown in Hindle's book. Ultimately the route led to Hawkeshead which, like Ravenglass, had a market. If so, this bridge would be on it as well as on a path over to Seathwaite. Another use would have been to carry packhorse trains from the slate quarries in the Dunnerdale Fells. Water Yeat means water gate, part of the apparatus of the water mill sited nearby. The bridge has a span of about six metres and a width of almost two metres and is said to date from the eighteenth century

28) *Wet Sleddale* (Gp 2) NY539109
There are lots of places in the Lake District that, with justification, could be called 'wet' and this is just one of them. The bridge was originally further down river but was dismantled and rebuilt by Manchester Corporation when it created Wet Sleddale reservoir. The original was said to be seventeenth century and connected farms in Wet Sleddale to Shap. It was without parapets but the rebuilt version has high parapets. Its span is about nine metres and its width almost two metres. The bridge crosses the main inlet to the reservoir formed by the confluence of Sleddale Beck and Tonguerigg Gill. To view it, park near the dam, which is reached by a side road from the A6 south of Shap, and walk along the path on the south side of the reservoir. There is then a path that branches off to the left and leads to the bridge.

29) *Widewath 1* (Gp 2) NY501208
There are two bridges crossing Heltondale Beck within about 100 metres of each other. Both are on private land. The first is some 200 metres or so south of Widewath Farm, down a wide green path with stone walls on each side. There is an an old well house on the right near the farm yard. Beyond a gate at the bottom of this path a rough track turns to the right and goes through some woodland as it descends to the beck. An alternative route is to park just beyond the disused water mill at Heltondale, clamber up the grassy bank and then walk upstream alongside the river to pick up a path that descends through some woodland to the bridge. It has a segmental arch almost three metres wide and about eight metres long with a low parapet on the downstream side and no parapet upstream. It is thought to be seventeenth century and was restored in 2006. Some of the water from this beck has been diverted into Haweswater via a tunnel. It does not appear to be on a known packhorse route and may have been used to provide access to fields.

30) *Widewath 2* (Gp 2) NY500208
The second bridge is just upstream from the first, near two ruined stone buildings. It is about three metres wide with a span of more than five metres. It is in good condition and has no parapets. A curving track leads down to it from the farm side of the beck but it is best reached by walking upstream on the track from Widewath 1. Again it was probably a farm bridge.

31) *Winster* (Gp 1) SD412943

I had some difficulty finding this bridge, the reason being that it is so close to the road and overgrown that it is easily missed. The wall at the side of the road is in the line of the near side of the bridge although it changes to railings for the length of the bridge. It is a simple arch without parapets and with arch stones exposed on its top surface. There are county records showing it to have been built in 1729 at a cost of £25. Its span is about two and a half metres and its width almost two metres. Presumably it was on a route now converted to the A5074 that would have run between Kendal and Ambleside. Fortunately this whole area managed to escape being flooded to create another reservoir in the 1960s.

OTHER INTERESTING BRIDGES

1) *Barnscar* SD134954

This bridge was listed by the National Park Authority in 1999 but when I visited (in May 2008) it had been demolished, presumably by the force of water coming down Black Beck. Its constituent stones could be seen a short distance downstream, illustrating the fate of some stone bridges. It was said to consist of three large boulders in the bed of the stream with two stone slabs laid on top of them forming the pathway with more stones placed at each end. It was five metres long, 0.9 metres wide and 0.6 metres above the water and was near to, but not on, a path from Ravenglass to Boot. Most, if not all, packhorse traffic must have gone via Eskdale Green as this would entail less effort. It was probably just to allow easy access to and from the fields to the south of the beck although when I visited the stream could be easily crossed by walking on the many boulders. Barnscar, curiously known as the City of Barnscar, was a major Bronze Age settlement and some ancient cairns and the remains of many buildings have survived. Readyhough lists nineteen Black Becks!

Although Barnscar itself is interesting to see, I do not feel that the remains of the bridge warrant a visit. When I went I had to clamber up a steep, wooded escarpment, without the benefit of any visible path although one was shown on the OS map. I started from a bend in the road just south of Muncaster Bridge. A path eventually appeared and some careful navigation, taking account of the walls marked on the OS map, was needed to reach Barnscar. The bridge, or its remains, are found downhill, pretty well due south of the settlement near to a new, makeshift bridge. There may be an easier way from Dyke but either hardly seem worth the effort.

2) *Bridge House*

This is probably the best-known bridge in the Lake District and for good reason. It is a little, two-roomed, house perched on a bridge over Stock Ghyll in the centre of Ambleside. The house was probably built in the seventeenth century as a summer house but has had various different lives, once housing a family with six children. I would rather not think about the logistics of their living arrangements. It is now owned by the National Trust and entry is free. It is a living, or at least stable, demonstration of how much weight a small, stone, arched bridge can take without showing the slightest sign of falling into the stream below. Try that on a stone beam.

Plate 11: Bridge House, Ambleside.

3) *Single span clapper bridge at Cawdale* NY491180

Not all stone beams are bad, they just have their limitations. This one is perfectly adequate as it has a small span and no one has built a house on it. They were easier to make than an arch as long as you could find and carry a hefty chunk of slate. To view the bridge go to Bampton and drive uphill on the narrow road towards High Hullockhowe. Continue on the road to Moorahill Farm. The bridge is about 150 metres south of the road across some boggy ground. It is marked as a foot bridge on the OS map and is about as perfect a clapper bridge as you can get. There is an arched bridge, Stanegarth, about 300 metres downstream.

Plate 12: Cawdale Clapper Bridge.

4) *Multi-span clapper bridges at Fusedale* NY445195

There are two, multi-span, clapper bridges over Fusedale Beck, quite close to each other, just off the narrow road heading uphill from Mellguards. The first is about halfway up in some woodland and has three spans, the two side spans being quite small. Its total length is about five metres and its maximum width rather less than two.

The second bridge is pretty much at the top of the hill in more open country. There is a path the short distance to it from a sign post to Swarthbeck. It has a single pier crudely fashioned to make a cutwater. It is about four metres long by one and a half wide.

These bridges illustrate the limitations of stone beams. Although this is not a wide stream the stone beams have to be supported by a pier or piers in the water. These crossings could easily have been bridged by small arches. Nevertheless they have served their purpose, no doubt for many years.

Plate 13: (upper) Fusedale Bridge

5) *Single piece stone arch over Barrow Beck* NY373295

This is an unusual bridge made from a single slab of slate which is quite thin and has a very shallow natural arch. Apart from the arch it has the appearance of a clapper bridge and the question is, does it function as a beam or an arch? For it to function as an arch it needs to be in compression, i.e. its ends must be firmly fixed. Close inspection of this bridge shows that one end is cemented into the roadway but the other is not. Neither end is built into the structure of the bridge in the way that a true arch bridge would be. In my view this is insufficient fixation for it to be called an arch and the bridge functions mainly as a beam.

To see it, take the road that goes north from the A66 between Penrith and Keswick, heading for Mungrisdale. About half a kilometre south of Low Beckside Farm, walk east across the fields on a path. After about half a kilometre the path crosses Barrow Beck on the bridge.

Plate 14: Bridge over Barrow Beck,

6) *Troutbeck Park* NY418067

Although this clapper bridge is on a little-used path in part of a valley that sees few visitors it is a large and impressive structure. It has no less than five waterways, the piers between which must cause considerable obstruction to the flow of water. It is almost nine metres long and four metres wide, far bigger than the ones in Fusedale. Troutbeck had packhorse routes going east to Kentmere over Garburn Pass, north to Ullswater over Kirkstone Pass and west to Ambleside along Robin Lane and south to Windermere. Kirkstone was the obvious route north so it is unlikely that this bridge was on a packhorse route which has now been forgotten. Bulmer in his *History, Topography, and Directory of Westmorland* (1885) says that each of the three Troutbeck Hundreds (about 1,200 acres) had a bridge, but it may be a more recent farm bridge to reach fields on the far side of Trout Beck. Alternatively, if it is old enough, it might have been used by medieval deer hunters. A nice thought. To visit the bridge see Short Walk 9, Troutbeck Church to Troutbeck Park Bridge, page126.

3: WALKS ALONG PACKHORSE ROUTES

To get from place to place in the early Lake District most people would have walked but this would have been impractical when heavy loads had to be carried. The first industry in the area, other than agriculture, was mining, whose products would have taxed the carrying power of any walker. Wheeled transport was probably only used around settlements. Packhorses, and sometimes sledges for downhill runs, were of more use over rough ground.

In the middle ages wool made England's wealth and the economy of the Lake District was no exception and packhorses were used extensively for its transport. They were organised in strings of up to 40 with panniers similar to the ones seen today. An original saddle can be seen in the restored water mill at Boot (see Burn Moor), together with a copy of what was the sign over the Packhorse Inn in Kendal showing a laden packhorse.

Plate 15: Packhorse saddle from Boot Mill.

A horse could carry up to about 100 kilograms and travel around 25 kilo-metres in a day. Occasionally they carried passengers, one young lady being considered to be the equivalent of half a pack. They were slow but fairly reliable and able to deal with rough ground under foot (or under hoof) as long as the steeper gradients were lessened by creating zigzags and the bigger streams crossed by bridges.

Some of what became packhorse routes had earlier origins. Kirkstone, Wrynose and Hardknott passes were Roman roads which became pack-horse routes and are now tarmac roads. There were also medieval roads, often associated with trade linked to the monasteries. Drove roads such as the one over Garburn Pass between Troutbeck and Kentmere and onto Sadgill were used for moving cattle and sheep. They developed during the late Middle Ages and were also used by packhorse trains. The Garburn drove road joined the old Roman road from Eskdale to Ambleside over Wrynose and Hardknott passes and then connected with the packhorse routes through Kentmere and Long Sleddale. Another type of route was the corpse road used to ferry the dead to the nearest burial ground. There are usually only one or two economical routes from valley to valley and it is not surprising that their state and use changed over the years.

By the middle of the eighteenth century Kendal had become the mar-keting centre of the woollen trade in the Lake District. According to Hindle more than twenty gangs of packhorses worked out of Kendal every week. Their memory is preserved in some public house names, such as the Pack Horse at Keswick and the Woolpack at Boot, Kendal and Keswick. Their routes were along valley bottoms, as long as they were not too wet, and over the passes between the valleys. They did not go over the tops of mountains or around the bottoms but took the best compromise between distance and climb, given the local topography. This makes them excellent routes for walkers who want to get from one valley or village to the next rather than conquer peaks. In general they were not engineered except to make the zigzags, or where crossing a bog was unavoidable, in which case large stones would be used.

Many of the best routes have been covered in tarmac and although they can be walked, it is not necessarily a pleasant, or safe, experience. Fortunately enough have been left untouched for the walker to enjoy and some of the more picturesque ones will be described. The drove roads and the sand roads (see Hindle) will not be covered except where they were also used as packhorse routes or provide links for the circular walks. The packhorse routes can be walked as detailed here, but the trouble is that they go from valley A to valley B while your car is still in valley A. Unless you are prepared to turn around and retrace your steps (well the view is different even if the path is the same) you have either to find another way home, such as a bus, do something in a group with two cars or stop overnight.

Those doing there-and-back walks, as I usually did, will face a minimum of two climbs, sometimes as many as four, and have to cover a fair

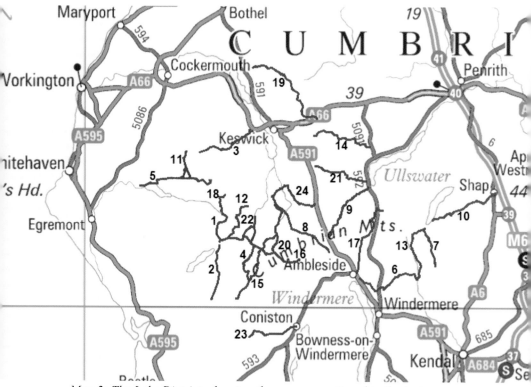

Map 2: The Lake District, showing the passes mentioned in the text.
© Crown Copyright and/or database right. All rights reserved. Licence number 100048757.

1) Black Sail Pass
2) Burn Moor
3) Coledale Hause
4) Esk Hause
5) Floutern Pass
6) Garburn Pass
7) Gatesgarth Pass
8) Greenup Edge
9) Grisedale Hause
10) Mardale Corpse Road
11) Mosedale
12) Moses Trod

13) Nan Bield Pass
14) Old Coach Road
15) Ore Gap
16) Rossett Gill Pass
17) Scandale Pass
18) Scarth Gap
19) Skiddaw
20) Stake Pass
21) Sticks Pass
22) Sty Head Pass
23) Walna Scar Road
24) Watendlath

distance. The individual climbs are not as long or as steep as those going up the mountains but added together they make a significant height gain, often more than climbing one of the peaks. The second climb is usually after lunch, and nobody should have to climb after lunch. Console your-self with the thought that at the end of one crossing there is always the pos-sibility of finding another way back if the weather turns nasty or your feet hurt. Another choice is just to do half the walk, turn around at the highest point of the pass and do the other half another day from the opposite end.

Some packhorse routes can be combined with a different way back, usu-ally with a short linking walk. These make good circular walks although again they can be quite long. Some of these will be described in Chapter 5 and you might think they make better outings. Inevitably there is some rep-etition as the same pass appears in different contexts although there is more detail in the descriptions of the pass walks. I have also listed some short walks, all of which include a bridge. These are more than just a walk to the bridge from the nearest bit of road but should not be too taxing.

The best way to get the most information about a particular walk is by looking up the route in all its different contexts. For example, parts of cir-cular walk 5, from Eskdale to Esk Hause, Sty Head, Wasdale Head, Burn Moor and then back to Eskdale are also described under circular walk 4, Esk Hause, Sty Head and Burn Moor passes and to some extent Ore Gap and Rossett Gill passes. To make this easier I have included notes to this effect on all the walks.

1) BLACK SAIL PASS (Wasdale Head Bridge)
(see also Burn Moor, Moses Trod, Scarth Gap, Sty Head Pass and circu-lar walk 2)
This pass goes from Wasdale Head to the floor of the Ennerdale Valley where it joins the route from Buttermere via Scarth Gap. You can walk over this pass by itself from Wasdale Head; alternatively you can combine it with Scarth Gap and start either at Wasdale Head or Buttermere, but it then has four climbs if you go there and back.

The origin of such a curious name as Black Sail for a pass is uncertain. Whaley thinks it may mean dark (not too hard), i.e. peaty, and the sail part to be a mire or puddle or alternatively a hollow or pass. A pass covered in peat does not seem too unreasonable.

Assuming you have chosen to do the long one from Buttermere, the Black Sail part starts on the floor of the Ennerdale Valley at the wooden foot bridge (1) over the River Liza just down from the Black Sail Hut. The path then climbs steeply up with Sail Beck on the left (2). The steepness of the climb up to the pass is relieved, but not much, by some zigzags.

There are some on the other side too but they never seem as important on the way down. The col (3) is at about 550 metres. The path to Pillar is on the right and that to Kirk Fell on the left. Straight ahead is Wast Water, a favourite spot for depositing bodies. The reason for this dubious honour is that it is the deepest lake at 76 metres but persons contemplating such an outing should take care to avoid the underwater shelf that caught out at least one murderer. Coniston is preferred by some but with no greater success (so far as we know).

Descending on the far side, Gatherstone Beck is crossed about halfway down (4). Hindle says there used to be a bridge here but there is no sign of it now. Eventually the valley floor is reached. This is one of the many Mosedales (q.v.) and has an impressive wall of big mountains surrounding most of it. At the bottom is the village of Wasdale Head with its photogenic stone walls and curiously-shaped fields. The path joins Moses Trod (5) which at this stage has already merged with the three paths from Sty Head. As the small village of Wasdale Head (6) is entered the path passes to the

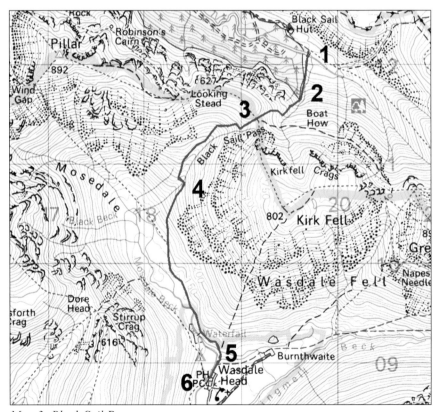

Map 3: Black Sail Pass.

Plate 16: Wasdale Head Bridge

left of the near-perfect packhorse bridge. The bridge is easy of access but is
not on the route. Either it had another purpose, such as to reach the fields
beyond, or the path has changed course. The latter would be nicer.

2) BURN MOOR (Wasdale Head and Boot bridges)
(see also Sty Head Pass, Black Sail Pass and circular walks 2 and 5)

The desire to be buried in consecrated ground meant that bodies had to be
moved from remote hamlets to the nearest church with a burial ground.
There are several such coffin or corpse roads in the Lake District and this
is one of them. The small church at Wasdale Head was only licensed for
burials in 1901 and before that the coffin and body had to be moved, either
on horseback or a light cart, to Boot in Eskdale. This must have been a sad
and rather macabre journey for all concerned over this wild and desolate
stretch of moorland. There is a legend that the moor is still haunted by a
horse that became lost in the mist while carrying a coffin and was never
found. As well as being used as a coffin road it also carried packhorse traffic between Wasdale Head and Boot.

Wasdale Head has arguably the most majestic setting of any village in
the Lake District, surrounded on three sides by Yewbarrow, Kirk Fell, Great
Gable, Lingmell and the Sca Fell range and on the fourth by Wast Water. It
has a shop, several farms, a famous climbing hotel, the Wasdale Head Inn,
and a small church, Saint Olaf's. As well as its climbing associations the

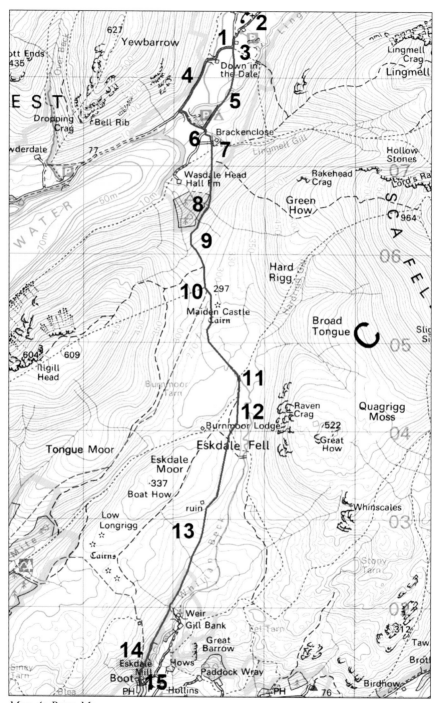

Map 4: Burn Moor.

© Crown Copyright and/or database right. All rights reserved. Licence number 100048757.

inn was the home of Will Ritson (1808 to 1890). He was born in what was
then a farmhouse which he extended and turned into the Huntsman's Inn
to cater for, in his words, "The idiots who walk the hills." As well as
befriending early mountaineers he achieved fame as a raconteur, becoming known as 'The world's greatest liar.' He is commemorated by Ritson's
bar in the hotel and by the annual 'World's Greatest Liar' competition held
at Santon bridge.

Saint Olaf's is set a small distance apart from the village but is worth a
visit. The village claims that it is the smallest church in England but this
is probably not so. The head stones in its church yard bear witness to several climbing accidents in the nearby hills. Wasdale means the valley of
the lake. Burn Moor might be a corruption of borran meaning ancient
remains and there are certainly some on the moor, particularly at Maiden
Castle, Boat How, Brat's Moss and alongside Whillan Beck.

Starting at Wasdale Head there is ample parking on the village green
just down the road from the village towards the lake (1). The church is a
short walk from here along a bridle way towards the head of the valley (2).
Going in the opposite direction, towards the pass, take the tarmac road
from the car park heading for the lake and where it turns to the right go
straight ahead and onto a wide path (3). It is sign-posted to Eskdale and
Miterdale. This path is liable to flooding and an alternative in doubtful
weather is to continue along the tarmac road (4) and then turn left at the
camp site. The first choice goes through a rather damp area called 'Down
in the Dale' and crosses a wide, stony river bed (5), presumably the site of
the flooding, before it reaches the camp site. Continue along the side of the
camp site and at the far end go through the middle of three gates (6) to start
a gentle climb through a small area of pleasant woodland with a climbing
hut called Brackenclose on the left (7).

Leaving the woodland, the wet and stony path climbs slowly between
fields and then goes alongside an area of mixed woodland called Fence
Wood (8) where it climbs more steeply. Along here is a new, double-
humped bridge with a curved roadway and parapets. It is good to see that
new bridges can be built in as attractive a fashion as old ones. Just after
the end of the wood the route turns to the left (9). This is cairned but is
easy to miss as the path ahead is clearer and more enticing. In fact route
finding is a problem over the whole of Burn Moor until the descent into
Boot. It is a wide, fairly-flat area with only a few unique identifying features and it is easy to wander off in the wrong direction. Provided you
realise what has happened the situation can usually be retrieved by walking across the moorland to the correct path but beware of bogs. If all else
fails just retrace your steps until you find the right path again.

The path continues to climb, but more gently now, with good views of Yewbarrow on the far side of Wast Water, until the summit of the pass is reached at a little over 290 metres (10). On the left, and reached by a short detour, is Maiden Castle, a Bronze Age remnant which is now just a ring of stones. Much further to the east is the enormous bulk of the Sca Fell range with its waterfalls, to the south is Eskdale Fell and to the west is Ill Gill Head. Burnmoor Tarn becomes visible ahead with a small house at its far end. These are two of the features useful for confirming that you are on the right track. The house is Burnmoor Lodge which was built as a fishing and hunting lodge but is now empty with its windows boarded up and looks rather forlorn. The tarn is the third largest in the Lake District and is owned by the National Trust.

Coming down towards the tarn there is a large, but tumbled down, sheep enclosure on the right of the path. Nearer the tarn the route goes over a wide, wet area of several small streams. Keeping the tarn on the right, go over a wooden footbridge called Bulatt Bridge (11). This is the origin of Whillan Beck, the outflow from the tarn, which is unusually close to its main inflow mentioned above. The path (12) continues to go south although there are others which go up Eskdale Moor and to the lodge. A little further on (at NY187042 according to Readyhough) is where the unfortunate horse carrying the coffin disappeared. Shortly afterwards there is a path off to the left which goes down to a foot bridge over Whillan Beck. This is not on our route but in clear weather is useful for confirming that you have selected the correct path.

The route (13) descends along a variable, and at times very wet, path towards Boot. Eventually walled fields are reached and Whillan Beck becomes enclosed in a wooded ravine behind a dry stone wall. The path is joined by another from Miterdale (14) and enters Boot (15) by the old water mill. This is open as a museum and is worth exploring to see its machinery. What's more it still works. Immediately after the mill is the packhorse bridge, well worth a look at. Boot has a few cottages, an hotel unsurprisingly called The Boot Inn, and a shop.

For walkers starting at Boot the path is easy to find at the end of the road just over the bridge and past the mill. There is no parking in the village apart from that provided for patrons of the hotel and residents. There is parking about half a kilometre away at the railway station at Dalegarth, down the road towards the coast. This is the Eskdale end of the famous Ravenglass and Eskdale narrow gauge steam railway. It was opened in 1875 to carry iron ore from the Eskdale mines to the coast but soon started to carry passengers as well. The line closed in 1913 when the mines closed but was bought by Bassett Lowke, the model engineer, in 1915. It

Plate 17: Boot Bridge and Mill.

is now run by a preservation society. One way the walk is about twelve kilometres long and takes around three hours.

Most people will probably start or finish the walk at Boot but, if you want to reach the church at the end of the coffin road, you have another kilometre to walk. Go down the road from Boot, cross the main valley road and continue along a wide track signposted to St. Catherine's, Eskdale Parish Church. The church is on the right, just before the river (see circular walk 5, pages 143 and 144).

3) COLEDALE HAUSE

The packhorse route between Braithwaite and Buttermere goes along the bottom of the wide Coledale Valley, then steeply over Coledale Hause and down a shorter V-shaped valley to Crummock Water. Wainwright says that nobody would call Coledale beautiful but I think that is a little unfair. At its top end it has undoubtedly been ravaged by the mining industry but it has a certain harsh majesty about it and the mountains hereabouts are as good as any. On the far side of the Hause the valley down to Crummock Water provides a complete change and a rather more difficult path to walk.

Starting at the Braithwaite end there is some street parking and a small car park beside the Methodist Institute just over the river. Head out of the town on the road to Whinlatter Pass (1), which starts beside the Royal Oak pub, and go up the hill with Coledale Beck on the left. A short distance up the hill take the second exit off to the left and walk along a path that leads into the valley (2). A little further up the hill there is some more parking space (3) and a wider path that contours round to join the first path. Yet another path leaves the upper end of this parking area and heads towards the top of the valley side and onto Grisedale Pike. If you find yourself walking along a ridge you have taken the wrong path.

The path, really a narrow road, along the valley side (4) was the main access route to the mines at the head of the valley and is almost level all the way. The mine buildings soon come into view straight ahead. Although it is a slight detour, industrial archaeologists will want to view what remains of it. This is the Force Crag Mine (5) which was the last working mineral mine in the Lake District. The present mine started in 1839 and closed in 1991. Some mining for silver and lead started in the area in the sixteenth century but the buildings you can see were constructed in 1908/9. The main shaft goes into the side of Grisedale Pike just behind the buildings and you can stoop down and go a short distance along the level until you meet a securely fastened gate. There is an impressive flow of red-coloured water emerging continuously through pipes below your feet, or at least there was when I visited. The mine was used to extract lead, zinc

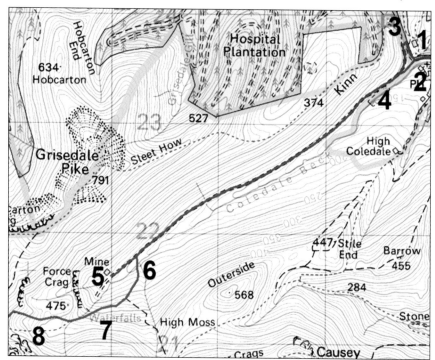

Map 5: Coledale Hause, east.

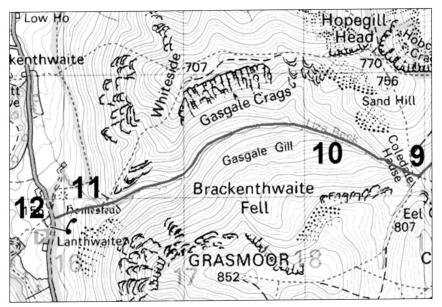

Map 6: Coledale Hause, west.

and latterly mainly barytes (barium sulphate, used in white paint). It is now owned by the National Trust and from time to time they have guided tours through the buildings.

The packhorse route turns off to the left before reaching the mine, and crosses the river (6) on stepping stones. It then ascends (7) to the left of Force Crag on an obvious but stony path. At the top of this climb there are some more stepping stones and to the right the remains of a small dam. Earlier OS maps show a more direct route through the mine area but this is invisible now and anyway would have led to a steep climb up some spoil. Continue on the clear path which zigzags up the hill (8) with more mine workings on the far right.

Eventually Coledale Hause is reached (9) and with it the path between Hopegill Head and Crag Hill, part of the walk called the Coledale Round. On a clear day the sea is visible in the distance. I once lost a hat up here. It was an exceptionally windy day and somewhere on the top of Crag Hill I opened my rucksack to extract a map. I had previously put my new Tilley Endurable in the sac to stop it blowing off my head but it immediately seized this opportunity for freedom and took off in the direction of the Coledale Valley with the dog and me in hot pursuit. The hat disappeared over the edge and the dog and I just managed to stop before we joined it. My walking friend, the dog and I then descended into the bowl below but could find no trace of the hat.

Keeping a tight grip on your hat go down the far side of the Hause along a narrow and at times eroded and precarious path into the V-shaped valley that holds Liza Beck (10). I had thought that Liza was the name of some long-forgotten young lady but it comes from the Old Norse words meaning 'light' and 'river'. Much of this path is on scree and its exact course probably changes as the scree moves. The path descends steeply at first and keeps close to the beck and then flattens out. To the right are the dark and forbidding Gasgale Crags between Hopegill Head and Whiteside. There are some ruined stone buildings just to the left of the path. As Liza Beck curves round to the left the path descends more steeply, keeping close to the river, and is rocky in places. As it is now it would have been difficult, if not impossible, for a packhorse train to negotiate. Perhaps the topography or the exact route has changed, or perhaps the trains moved from side to side over the beck, which is quite narrow and would not have posed much of an obstacle.

Suddenly the valley opens out (11) and Crummock Water can be seen in the distance. After crossing the beck on a wooden bridge there is a pleasant, wide, grassy path down to Lanthwaite Green Farm (12) and the road to Buttermere. If you start at this end there is a car park here. One way, the route is about nine kilometres and takes around two and a half hours, depending on how extensive is your tour of the mine.

4) ESK HAUSE (Lingcove Bridge, possibly Stockley Bridge)
(see also circular walks 4 and 5 and short walk 4)

Boot, in Eskdale, had several packhorse routes out to the north and east. Two led to Rosthwaite in the Borrowdale Valley via the valley where the River Esk is joined by Lingcove Beck. These are the passes called Ore Gap and Esk Hause. Although not the highest pass in the Lake District, Mickledore between Sca Fell and Scafell Pike and Ore Gap are higher, Esk Hause is considered to be the highest pass that was in regular use by the packhorse trains. Hause means a neck of land, ridge or col between valleys, so Esk Hause is the col where the Esk originates.

Boot itself has two bridges of note, one in the centre next to an old water mill and the other, the Doctor Bridge, a kilometre or so along the road to the east. The first part of the route is along this road, albeit further to the east. It is now tarmac but was originally a packhorse road. This leads to the notorious Hardknott and Wrynose passes. These have the narrowest and steepest (1 in 3, 33%) roads with the sharpest bends and the biggest drops in the Lake District and are best avoided by drivers of a nervous disposition. Just before the road starts to climb to the first of these passes there is a grassy parking space beside the road (1). As parking in Boot is

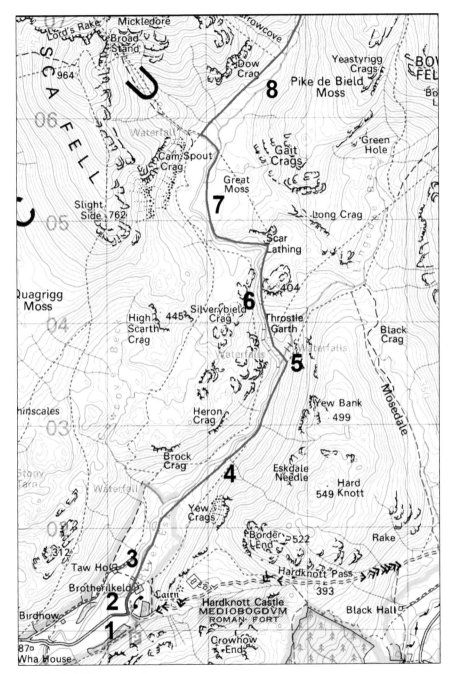

Map 7: Esk Hause, south.

well nigh impossible and the walk along the road is tedious, it seems reasonable to start here.

Leaving the parking area go along the road towards Hardknott Pass. The route to Esk Hause leaves to the left a short distance along this road by a telephone kiosk and heads towards the river along a farm road (2). The footpath starts (3) almost at the end of this road and squeezes between the River Esk and Brotherikeld Farm. This path (4), which is always obvious, continues at a varying distance from the river for about three kilometres, rising very slowly. About half way along, on the skyline to the right, is the Eskdale Needle. This is an impressive, isolated rock, about fifteen metres high on its Eskdale side but has never achieved the fame of its colleague on Great Gable.

Eventually the path reaches Lingcove Bridge (5). This is a perfect packhorse bridge in a perfect setting. It even has a waterfall upstream. After admiring it from all angles go over the bridge and climb the path straight ahead (6), going pretty well due north with the River Esk in an increasingly deep ravine on the left. At the top of this climb the river curves to the right and the path follows it around. It crosses a small boggy area at the western end with Crinkle Crags visible to the east and then passes under Scar Lathing and turns another corner to reach the large, boggy bowl of The Great Moss (7).

The path here is difficult to follow and can be very wet underfoot. It was around here that Robert Orrell almost lost one of his packhorses when doing

Plate 18: Lingcove Bridge.

his long trek over the Lake District passes. In fact there are several paths, some on small causeways, and mostly not shown on the OS map. Some trial and error may be needed to make your way across this large obstacle and I have never managed the same route twice. There are no bridges across the

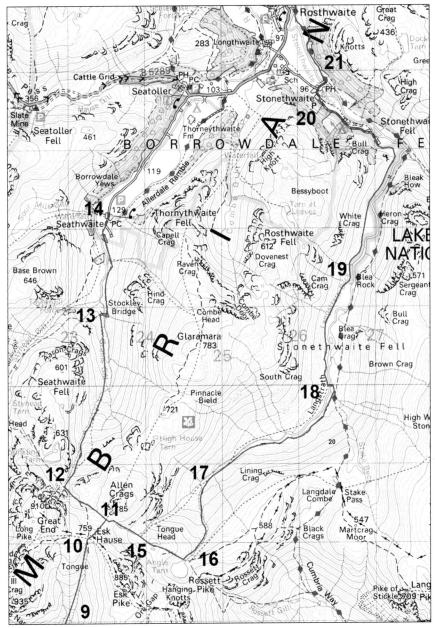

Map 8: Esk Hause, north.

river but it is fairly shallow and easy to ford at several places and should not present too much of a problem. Although I do not generally use walking poles they can be very useful for retaining one's balance while crossing rivers and I should thank the group of four young men who were returning from a night on Scafell Pike who kindly lent me one of theirs.

One way or another the far side of the river is reached and the path moves in a north easterly direction along the base of the Scafell Pike range (8). I once found several pieces from a wrecked aircraft around here. The fragments were small and it was impossible to say whether they were from a helicopter or something with wings, but they served as a reminder that mountains have never been the friends of aircraft, particularly when instrumentation was not as good as it is today.

The path crosses Little Narrowcove and climbs up along a tongue of glacial moraine to reach a narrow and rocky gully (9) with a small stream running through it which must have proved something of a challenge to the packhorses. At the top of this is Esk Hause (10) at 759 metres and the view opens out with Great End to the left, Esk Pike to the right and Allen Crags, the beginning of the Glaramara range, straight ahead.

The path then descends to the great walkers' highway (11) between Great Gable and the Langdale Valley. This, too, was a packhorse route, from Wasdale Head to the Langdale Valley and on to Ambleside. Our route probably turned left here, towards, but not as far as, Sprinkling Tarn, and then turned right towards Borrowdale. The made-up path starts on the far side of a small stream and follows the edge of Ruddy Gorge (12), so called because of its red-coloured rock. The path is rocky and steep at times and crosses Ruddy Gill on a modern wooden bridge about half way down. It descends to join another packhorse route which has come from Wasdale over Sty Head Pass. Very shortly after this, the path crosses Stockley Bridge (13), another packhorse bridge, albeit a rebuilt one. It continues along a wide, almost flat, path to Seathwaite (14). After the farm the path becomes a road which eventually joins the main road running along the floor of the Borrowdale Valley. Turning right here Rosthwaite is about two kilometres further on but most walkers will stop at Seathwaite for tea and cakes. Those choosing to start at Seathwaite will find ample parking alongside the road to the farm.

An alternative is to turn right rather than left after the descent from Esk Hause and walk in the direction (15) of the Langdale Valley. Hindle shows a packhorse route descending on the left to Langstrath between Allen Crags and Tongue Head, just to the right of Allencrags Gill, but a more obvious route, at least now, is alongside Angletarn Gill, the outlet from Angle Tarn. This path (16) goes to the left of the gill and crosses it further down to reach the valley floor. It then goes along the right bank (17) of Langstrath Beck and joins the route over Stake Pass (18). There are then paths on both sides of the river and either will do. Once reached, the valley floor is pretty much flat all the way to Stonethwaite. The paths converge, but do not join, at Blackmoss Pot (19), a deep and cold pool favoured by the more adventurous swimmers, and then part company again until bridges join them at Johnny House and again at Stonethwaite. There is limited parking at Stonethwaite (20) but there is a pub and an excellent cottage tea shop. Rosthwaite is further down the valley either on roads or across the bridge and along the much more pleasant path (21) on the far side of Stonethwaite Beck, now part of the Cumbria Way.

Whichever final pathway is chosen this is a long walk. It takes about three and a half hours from Eskdale to Esk Hause and another two to Seathwaite or another four to Stonethwaite which makes a one-way walk to Seathwaite about five and a half hours and to Stonethwaite about seven and a half. Too far for there-and-back walks. A better plan is just to do a one way crossing, or walk up to the pass and then return and do the other end another day. Alternatively do one of the circular walks that includes Esk Hause.

5) FLOUTERN PASS
(see Mosedale Pass, and circular walk 1)
Floutern Pass is named after the tarn which is about half way between Ennerdale Bridge and Buttermere, in fact the 'tern' part of Floutern means tarn. The origin of the 'flou' part is obscure. The packhorse route would

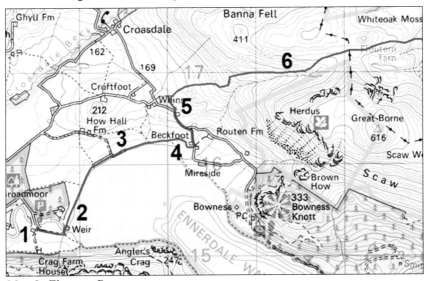

Map 9: Floutern Pass.

have started at Ennerdale Bridge and probably followed what is now a tar-mac road to Whins. A more pleasant alternative is to start at the car park by Bleach Green Cottages (NY085153) (1), walk along the path to the lake and then turn left to follow the lake side (2). About one and a half kilometres along this path there is a route up to Whins which is marked on the OS map but it is overgrown and difficult to find (3). It leads to a nar-row, fenced path up a field to the road leading to Whins. It is easier to spot from this end. Judging from the notices on the barn adjacent to the top end of the path its history is not a happy one.

A longer, but easier to navigate, alternative, at least in this direction, is to go a little further round the foot of the lake. Where the path turns sharply to the right to follow the lake shore (4), go straight ahead along an enclosed track to Beckfoot and then turn left to go up the hill to join the road to Whins. At the top of the hill, before reaching Whins, where the road turns left, take the path on the right, sign-posted "Buttermere 4½ miles" (5). This goes uphill along a stoney and enclosed path. It is shortly

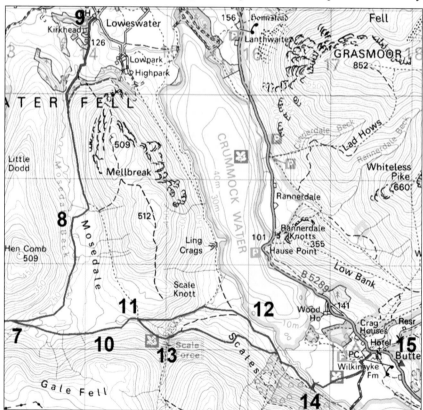

Map 10: Floutern Pass.

joined by the other path from Whins and heads into more open country with Gill Beck and Herdus to the right and Banna Fell to the left (6). The path is fairly clear and eventually at the top of the pass, at about 410 metres, Floutern Tarn appears to the right. Continue on the path past the tarn and shortly after a sheepfold on the right, the path forks (7).

The left fork goes to one of the Lake District's many Mosedales and onto Loweswater. This was also a packhorse route and this path connects with the route going between Buttermere and Loweswater. The path is wet and at times difficult to follow as it skirts round the side of Hen Comb and then crosses the valley floor, but at least the major obstacle, Mosedale Beck, is crossed by a metal bridge (8). Once the route on the far side of Mosedale is reached the path is clear and dry and takes a pleasant, gentle descent into the village of Loweswater (9).

The alternative is to take the right fork. Do not go straight ahead. I once did this by mistake and found myself in a bog from which I thought I was not going to emerge alive (or at all). Follow the path on the right that heads towards a wooden gate. Even this path is pretty wet and several small streams have to be crossed but eventually it becomes drier as the base of Gale Fell is reached (10). Continue on this path passing some ruined stone buildings higher up on the right. At the mouth of the valley descend to Black Beck (11) and follow the path on its far side down to Crummock Water (12). Alternatively take a shorter route by keeping to the right above Black Beck (13) and traversing round the side of Gale Fell crossing Scale Force at the wooden footbridge to join the more-travelled path from Red Pike. There are then various paths going down to the right, eventually reaching almost to the lakeside. This path is stony and, you will not be surprised to hear, wet in places. Follow the path as far as Scale Bridge (14) and then turn left over the bridge and follow the wide and clear path between the fields to the village of Buttermere (15).

Buttermere had packhorse routes to Lorton, to Braithwaite via Coledale or Newlands, and over Honister to Borrowdale, but by this time it is probably of more interest to know that it has two hotels if you feel that the return journey is just too much on the same day. For hardier souls there are two tea shops and the prospect of wet feet again on the way back. One way to Buttermere or Loweswater takes about three hours and is about twelve kilometres.

6) GARBURN PASS
(see Nan Bield Pass and circular walk 8)
Garburn Pass links the villages of Troutbeck and Kentmere. Troutbeck had a branch over Kirkstone Pass and probably linked with Ambleside along what is called Robin Lane on the OS map, and Kentmere had links to

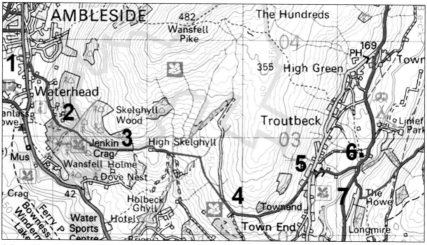

Map 11: Garburn Pass, west.

Mardale over Nan Bield Pass, and Sadgill in Long Sleddale.

If you want to start from Ambleside there are several car parks in the town but the nearest to the start of the route is along the road that leads to Windermere (the A591), across the road from the garden centre. Walk towards Windermere for a short distance and then turn left immediately after the Mountain Rescue building (1). There is a sign pointing uphill to Skelghyll Wood and Jenkin Crag. Go along this narrow road ignoring the various turn offs to houses on the left. It becomes less of a road and more of a rocky path as it gets higher and enters the woods (2) but it is always clear and is well sign-posted. Eventually the path emerges from the woods and goes through the yard of High Skelghyll Farm (3). It then descends to cross a stream and climbs again to be joined from the left by the Hundreds Road (4). This was a drove road to the Troutbeck Hundreds. In medieval times a Hundred was the area of land that covered a hundred hides, a hide being the amount of land that would support a peasant family. Troutbeck had three Hundreds, Upper, Middle and Lower.

The path gradually curves round to the left and descends towards the village of Troutbeck (5), becoming a narrow tarmac road where the cottages begin. Where this narrow road joins a larger one, turn left past the Post Office and almost immediately turn right and head downhill past a farm building with a spinning gallery in its yard. The road is sign-posted to the church and descends quite steeply towards the river in the valley bottom, called, not surprisingly, Trout Beck.

If you choose to start at Troutbeck, to go either to Ambleside or

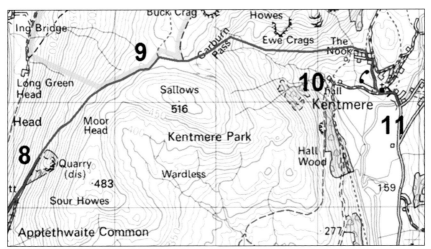

Map 12: Garburn Pass, east.

Kentmere, there is some parking space by the side of the river, near the church (6). If you are heading for Kentmere via Garburn Pass then turn right at the end of the road by the sixteenth century Jesus Church. This is well worth a visit in itself. Its large east window was the work of three of the Pre-Raphaelites, Edward Burne-Jones, Ford Maddox Brown and William Morris, who were said to have come to Troutbeck on a fishing holiday.

The route over Garburn leaves the A592, the road coming down from Kirkstone and going past the church, about 250 metres south of the church (7). There is a sign post saying 'public bridleway' leading up a stony path enclosed on both sides by dry stone walls. It climbs up past some build-ings on the right, collectively called The Howe, and an overgrown walled garden on the left. The path then turns to the left and shortly afterwards is crossed by Longmire Road, another path that goes along the side of the Troutbeck Valley. Not long afterwards, as it gently climbs the hillside, the path is joined by Dubbs Road, another track. Just up from this, on the right, is one of the Lake District's many disused quarries (8), screened from the road by some trees. Devotees of ruined quarries will want to admire what is left of its light railway, many excavations and spoil heaps. It has latterly become the home of two mobile telephone masts. These are never things of beauty and one wonders why companies cannot share masts and so reduce the visual pollution they produce but at least here they are well hidden. The path below the quarries appears quite threatened by the enormous spoil heap above it, which looks as if it is about to career down the hillside and submerge the walker in a torrent of slate.

The track, always obvious, continues to climb steadily until it reaches the apex of the pass at 447 metres, close to Garburn Nook (9). The path off to the left is the start of the Kentmere Round which traces out the watershed of the Kentmere Valley. Kentmere itself is a reservoir with a dam at its southern end. A little further on, Kentmere Valley comes into view and the track over to Sadgill can be seen on the far side. The path then descends towards Kentmere Village. Lower down on the right is the fourteenth century pele tower of Kentmere Hall (10) where Bernard Gilpin, known as the Apostle of the North, was born in 1517. He was educated at Queen's College, Oxford and ordained there in 1542 and became a fierce critic of the Church. Because of this, proceedings were twice started against him. On the second occasion he only escaped martyrdom by breaking his leg while travelling to London, thereby delaying his arrival, by which time Queen Mary's death had freed him from danger. Another Gilpin, Richard, is said to have killed the last wild boar in England. A doubtful honour. The tower is now uninhabited but is attached to a farm house. Its outside can be inspected by a short detour further down.

The long thin Kentmere Tarn can also be seen to the right, further down the valley. Originally there was a larger lake here which was drained over 150 years ago to provide pasture land. It was later discovered that the bed of the lake contained deposits of diatomite. These minute organisms contain silica which can be used in abrasives. This was extracted on a

Plate 19: Kentmere Hall.

commercial scale until the 1980s. The aerial ropeway, shown on the OS map, carried buckets of the dredged material down to the processing plant.

As Kentmere village is approached there is a large boulder in the field on the right. This is the Badger Rock or Brock Stone. There is access to it across the field for climbers who wish to polish their skills at a conveniently low level. A little further on the church of Saint Cuthbert is reached, again worth a look inside (11).

For people starting from the Kentmere end there is some parking around the Kentmere Institute, across the road from the church. There are signposts to Garburn Pass. For those doing the round trip from Troutbeck there is a seat for lunch just below the church. One way, the walk takes about an hour and a half.

7) GATESCARTH PASS
(see circular walks 8 and 9, and short walk 5)
Gatescarth, 'the mountain pass frequented by goats', and not to be confused with the similar-sounding Gatesgarth in Buttermere, links Mardale with Longsleddale. It is the sixth highest pass in the Lake District. Just down from the top it joins an old drove road to Swindale and Wet Sleddale. Further towards Longsleddale it becomes a quarry road. Sleddale means the 'valley with a side valley' or possibly it was a valley called Slaed. It was Long Whindale in Mrs Humphrey Ward's *Robert Elsmere* (1888) and Greendale in John Cunliffe's *Postman Pat* books (1993). Mardale means the 'valley with the lake', meaning Haweswater.

Starting at the Mardale end there is a small car park (1) and some parking along the road. Leaving the car park there are three paths, take the left hand one heading pretty much south beside some woodland. It soon climbs quite steeply as a rough stony path zigzagging up with Gatescarth Beck on the left (2). The pass reaches a maximum height of 594 metres at which point (3) a path leaves to the right to go up Little Harter Fell and then Harter Fell itself. Harter refers to a hart or stag. Continue on the clear path as it goes down the far side, in places quite steeply. On the right are the remains of Wrengill Quarry (4) with Wren Gill running through them. This is one of the oldest of the Lake District slate quarries, possibly the oldest. There are more quarries to the left of the path and further on into Mosedale. As the path levels out the route to Mosedale and onto Swindale and Wet Sleddale goes off to the left, almost at a right angle (5).

The Gatescarth path continues south and goes over a small bridge with a slate name plate underneath commemorating Denys Beddard. The path then begins its descent to Longsleddale on the quarry road. This is a wide, walled and engineered road although again quite steep in places (6). Wren

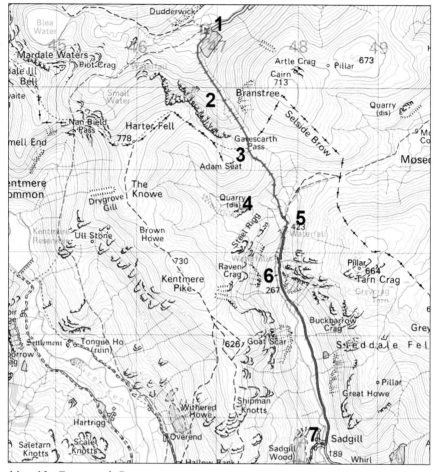

Map 13: Gatesgarth Pass.

Gill has now become the River Sprint and cascades down in a small ravine
on the right. Eventually the valley floor is reached and the path is more or
less flat all the way to Sadgill (7). Just before Sadgill the path becomes a
tarmac road.

Sadgill was an important packhorse junction connecting Kendal,
Mardale, Kentmere, Ullswater and Ambleside and it is not surprising that
a bridge was built here to make safe passage. It was constructed in 1717
and later widened. Look underneath and you can see the join. Sadgill
means 'the ravine or stream by the shieling' (grazing ground). There is
parking alongside the road at Sadgill but no tea shops at either end, sadly.
One way the walk is about six kilometres long and takes approximately
two and a half hours.

8) GREENUP EDGE
(see short walk 2 and circular walks 6 and 12)

Wordsworth has made Grasmere one of the best known of all the Lake District villages. For all that, it is rarely crowded in the way that Bowness can be and largely retains its peaceful beauty. Several packhorse routes started and finished in Grasmere. One went to Keswick over Dunmail Raise but this is now a busy road. Another went to Patterdale over Grisedale Hause and will be described later, and a third, perhaps the prettiest, led to Rosthwaite via Greenup Edge. There are several car parks in Grasmere, including one in a school yard that can be used at the weekends and during school holidays.

The route over Greenup Edge leaves Grasmere (1) along the road to Easedale which starts opposite the village green and Sam Read's bookshop. It continues along this road, passing an area of woodland where the path to Easedale Tarn leaves on the left (2). It then heads off to Far Easedale going between two fields (3) then some houses to turn right up a rough, enclosed, stony path. At the top of this short path, go through a gate and turn left. On the right, but invisible through the trees, is the famous Helm Crag which has on its summit the even-more-famous 'Lion and the Lamb' and the 'Old Lady Playing the Organ'. These large lumps of rock, which are separate, are easy to identify from a distance but surprisingly hard when close up. Any such examination would be a distraction from the

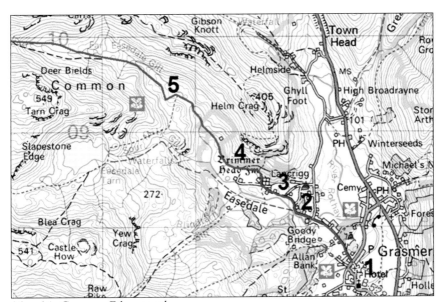

Map 14: Greenup Edge, south.

Map 15: Greenup Edge, north

planned route and would certainly not have been entertained by the packhorse drivers.

At first the path is stony and enclosed by walls and at times doubles as
a stream. As the path opens out Brimmer Head farm is on the left (4). It is
on this farm's ground that Willie Goodwaller's bridge is to be found. It is
not visible from this path however and is on private land. It is best seen
from a short stretch of the path up to Easedale Tarn (see Short Walk 2, Far
Easedale from Grasmere, page 114). The path along the Far Easedale valley floor is a good one although wet in places. Half way along the valley
it crosses Far Easedale Gill on a narrow wooden beam bridge (5), a much
more recent creation than the packhorse route. The valley continues for
some two kilometres before rising fairly steeply to the ridge at its far end
(6). After the ridge the ground dips to form a wet basin with a small river
running across it. This would not have caused too much of a problem to

the packhorses but can present a challenge to those of us who prefer to keep our feet dry. One possibility here is a deviation to the left keeping to higher ground.

On the far side of the basin the path rises again to Greenup Edge (7) and the high point of the route at about 610 metres. As is so often the case at a watershed the path is boggy with murky pools needing to be bypassed but improves considerably as it descends towards Stonethwaite and ultimately Rosthwaite. This descent is a delight with a large rocky outcrop about halfway down, called Lining Crag (8), on which to rest and take in the view down towards Stonethwaite. The route passes to the right of this outcrop down a steep and rocky path and then continues more gently down with Greenup Gill on the left. The path is always easy to follow. The descent is made even more delightful by the knowledge that all the hard climbing is over (at least if you are just going one way) and that with any luck tea and cakes are waiting in Stonethwaite. There is even a nice river there to water the horses, should you need it. At the bottom of the descent (9) the path to Stonethwaite goes for about a kilometre and a half along the right bank of the beck (10) and then across a bridge when the village (11) is reached. If you want to go on to Rosthwaite, just continue along the riverside path for another kilometre and then cross over. One way this walk is about eleven kilometres and takes about three hours.

9) GRISEDALE HAUSE
(see also circular walk 3)
Another packhorse route out of Grasmere is over Grisedale Hause to Patterdale and Ullswater. The route starts along what is now the road to Keswick but was then the important packhorse route over Dunmail Raise. Most walkers will no doubt wish to avoid the trudge along the road from Grasmere and there is a convenient parking place (1) about 500 metres from where the path starts, along the road towards Keswick. Coming from this car park the path goes off to the left at Mill Bridge (2), opposite the entrance to a minor road to Goody Bridge. It is sign-posted 'To Patterdale'.

The path proceeds upwards along an enclosed lane with Tongue Gill in a wooded ravine on the right. About 300 metres or so along this path there is a padlocked metal gate in the wall on the left, at the top of a few slate steps. This betrays the position of the Thirlmere to Manchester aqueduct which crosses Tongue Gill at the bottom of its steep-sided ravine at this point. After about three quarters of a kilometre the path opens up and there is a choice of routes (3) which go up either side of The Great Tongue. The left path is a little longer and has more height gain, the right climbs more slowly at first but then quite steeply towards the end. Hindle says the main route was to the left, perhaps for the horses to avoid the steep climb at the end of the alternative.

Going to the left, then, there is a wide grassy path with Little Tongue Gill at first on the left and then half way up, on the right. There are some minor zigzags as the path climbs (4). At the top of this climb the path turns to the right between Hause Riggs and Seat Sandal, levels, and then goes down a little. The alternative route is visible in the valley below but at this point has most of the climb to do, mainly on a made-up stone path. The

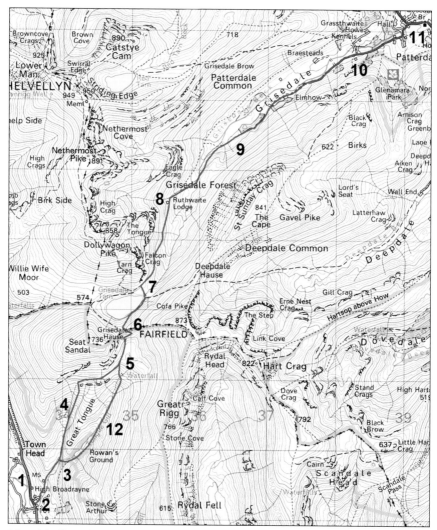

Map 16: Grisedale Hause.
© *Crown Copyright and/or database right. All rights reserved. Licence number 100048757.*

paths eventually join (5) and go north with the bowl of Hause Moss, the source of Tongue Gill, on the right. There is another, relatively short, zigzag to the top of the pass at Grisedale Hause at 588 metres (6).

Grisedale Tarn is now clearly visible ahead. Like so many mountain tarns Grisedale is devoid of trees or of anything much else. It is, however, one of the deepest at 35 metres and is said to contain the crown of Dunmail, King of Strathclyde. There are paths on either side but that on the right is more direct and more likely to have been the packhorse route. The stream leaving the tarn is crossed (7) on some stepping stones or just forded. The route then climbs a little to join the path to and from Dollywaggon Pike. This is an interesting name and I had long thought that it must refer to some wheeled contrivance that had been used on this mountain but Whaley says that the name "continues to defy explanation". It might just be a name, it might refer to a now-unknown Dorothy, or it might be a wagon. It looks an unlikely place to run wagons but it's a nice thought all the same.

Just to the right of the path here is the Brothers Parting Stone (marked on the OS map as such). The brothers referred to are William and John Wordsworth and the stone is a memorial to the place where they last saw each other on 29 September 1800. Some years later John's ship sank and there were no survivors. There is an inscription on the rock which is now all but illegible. It was placed there at the request of Canon Rawnsley, one of the founders of the National Trust, and consists of eight lines from Wordsworth's poem *In memory of my brother, John Wordsworth*.

The route then starts the descent to reach the floor of the long Grisedale Valley. About halfway down is a climbing hut called Ruthwaite Lodge (8). It was originally a smithy and a hut for miners from the nearby Eagle Crag and Ruthwaite Lodge mines and subsequently a shooting lodge when the mines closed in about 1880. It is in a lovely and well-chosen spot with a fine view down the valley and an impressive mountain behind it. Continue down on the clear path. There is a branch off to the left but the main route is straight ahead and shortly afterwards it crosses Grisedale Beck on a wooden footbridge (9). Grisedale is the valley where young pigs graze and at one time may have had a forest where hunting took place. The tree cover is pretty limited now but there are one or two patches of pleasant, mixed forest.

The path continues along the valley floor through fields and past farm buildings, some of which are now holiday lets. On the left, on the far side of the valley, is the path providing the long slog up to 'Hole in the Wall' on the way to Striding Edge and Helvellyn. There actually used to be a hole in the wall but now it is just a mundane stile. Eventually a tarmac road is reached (10) and this descends quite steeply to Patterdale and the road along the Ullswater Valley floor (11). There is some limited parking here.

One way the walk is about eleven kilometres and takes around three and a half hours. If you go both ways it might be nice to try the path on the other side of The Great Tongue on the way back (12). It is easy to follow and after the initial steepish descent is an easy walk out.

10) MARDALE CORPSE ROAD
(see also circular walks 8 and 9)

In the 1930s the village of Mardale Green was first demolished and then submerged beneath the surface of a Haweswater much expanded by the creation of a dam at its north-eastern end. Mardale had a corpse or coffin road leading from it to the church at Shap. This was to carry the dead of Mardale to be buried in the nearest consecrated ground before Mardale had its own burial ground in 1728 at Holy Trinity Church. Its last recorded use as a corpse road was in 1736, presumably for someone who had wished to be buried with predeceased relatives in Shap. The body would be carried over the back of a horse for the eight or so miles over the fells, sometimes in a coffin, sometimes not.

This is not the only corpse road in the Lake District. There is another, now of tarmac, leading from Rydal to Grasmere and passing in front of Dove Cottage. Just up the hill from Dove Cottage is a large stone (marked) where the pall bearers could place the coffin while they rested. Presumably no such convenience was provided for the horses used on the Mardale

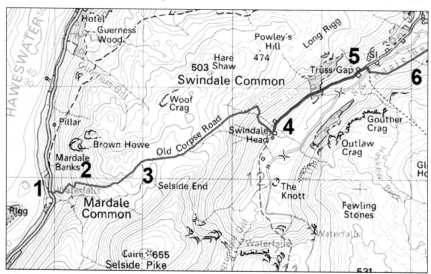

Map 17: Mardale Corpse Road, west.
© Crown Copyright and/or database right. All rights reserved. Licence number 100048757.

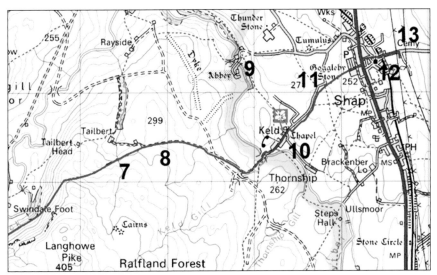

Map 18: Mardale Corpse Road, east.

road. Another such road is from Wasdale Head to Eskdale via Burn Moor (q.v. and Circular Walk 5, see page 142). Although these routes are known as corpse roads they were also used contemporaneously as packhorse routes.

The first part of the Mardale corpse road is submerged and can only be seen in a severe drought. It started at Holy Trinity Church in the middle of the village near to Chapel Bridge which has largely survived, albeit underwater. The path can be picked up (1) opposite 'The Rigg' on the motor road that passes alongside the eastern border of Haweswater. This was built by Manchester Corporation when the old road on the west side of the lake was submerged. There is a small car park here. The path is sign-posted to Swindale, another valley where pigs graze. It zigzags up (2) as a peat road (i.e. used for horses or sledges carrying peat) with the long waterfall of Rowantreethwaite Beck on the right. Towards the top it passes the ruins of several stone huts, formerly used for storing and drying peat, until it reaches Mardale Common.

On top the path (3) is wet in places but is well marked with posts. It rises to over 480 metres before descending towards Swindale, gently at first and then more steeply. It doubles back on itself to reach the end (or the start) of the road that runs along the valley floor (4). The tarmac road follows the old route as far as Truss Gap (5) (a farm, truss means a gap or narrowing) and then the corpse road parts company to ford Swindale Beck. There are now stepping stones here but feet can more reliably be kept dry

Plate 20: Ruined peat house on the Mardale Corpse Road with Haweswater in the background.

by using a foot bridge a bit further down stream. Whichever is chosen, the ground on the far side of the river is very wet, but the dry path is quickly reached a little further up the side of the valley.

After the stepping stones the path divides into two. The right fork goes over to Wet Sleddale, home to a packhorse bridge relocated and rebuilt by Manchester Corporation to avoid the fate of its colleagues at Mardale Green. The left fork (6) slowly climbs the side of Swindale Valley to its far end. In places the path appears engineered and is certainly well graded although sometimes a little wet. At the end of the valley the path turns east and goes alongside a stone wall south of Tailbert Farm and Dog Hill (7). At places the path is very wet and indistinct but it eventually meets an unfenced farm road (8) just past some farm buildings on the left. Turn right on this road. Shortly afterwards the remains of Shap Abbey (9) come into view to the north. Shap Abbey was founded by the Premonstratensians or White Canons in about 1199 and became a sizeable establishment. It was dissolved in 1540 and fell into ruin. Later on the farm road is crossed by a private waterworks road.

The corpse road continues over the River Lowther on a recent, and uninspired, bridge to Keld (10). The river marks the boundary of the National Park at this point. Keld is a small and rather pretty village with its own (sixteenth century) chapel. This was not the final destination of the cortege because it did not have a burial ground. It is now only occasionally used for services. The route follows the road out of Keld, or on a path close by it over a stone stile, and then alongside the wall in the field to the right of the road. It forks to the right at a public footpath sign (11) to go more directly towards Shap.

Closer to Shap the path passes a standing stone, originally part of the prehistoric Shap Avenue which was described as a, "stupendous monument of antiquity" consisting of "two lines of huge obelisks of unhewn granite" about 25 metres apart, leading to a stone circle about a mile away. The word 'Shap' means a heap or pile of stones, presumably these. The old road ends at the parish church of St Michael (12), almost in the centre of Shap. Beyond the church and over the railway bridge is the new burial ground for the dead of Mardale (13). The walk from Mardale in one direction takes about three and a half hours.

11) MOSEDALE
(see also Floutern Pass and circular walk 1)
There are several Mosedales in the Lake District and Readyhough lists four valleys, Swindale, Duddon, Wasdale and Loweswater and five becks. The Mosedale we are interested in is between the village of Loweswater and Floutern Pass with its packhorse route going on to Buttermere. Floutern itself was also a packhorse route, between Buttermere and Ennerdale, and is listed separately. Mosedale means 'the valley with a bog' and this one certainly lives up to (or down to) its name.

Buttermere (1) is a small village with two tea shops and two hotels, the Fish Hotel and the Bridge Hotel. The former is famous for having been the home of Mary Robinson, the 'Beauty of Buttermere' the story of whom is related in Melvyn Bragg's novel *The Maid of Buttermere*. She was a local lass who was tricked into marrying a bigamist called John Hatfield in 1802. He met his end a year later by being hanged at Carlisle, having been found guilty of forgery after a trial lasting all of eight hours. Mary later found a more satisfactory husband. The Bridge Hotel was originally a corn mill. There is some parking alongside the road to the Newlands Valley, although it is on something of a slope. There are other, official, car parks as well.

Leave Buttermere by the path alongside the car park of the Fish Hotel, turn left at the end and follow the path as it turns again (2) towards the far shore of the lake, between the fields of the land bridge dividing Buttermere and Crummock Water. At the end of this path (3) there is a stone bridge (Scale Bridge) crossing Buttermere Dubs, the river connecting the two

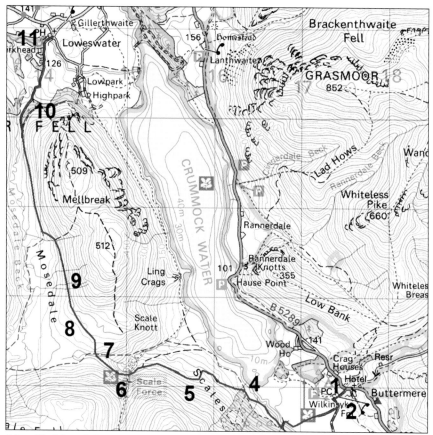

Map 19: Mosedale.

lakes. Go over the bridge and turn right along a stony path that is wet in places (4). To the left is the fell side leading up to Red Pike and to the right marshy grassland takes over from the fields. Continue on the path as Crummock Water becomes visible on the right.

There are several paths along here, the lowest keeping close to the lake side but the shortest route (5) moves diagonally up the hillside to cross Scale Beck over a wooden foot bridge (6) just below its waterfall. Over the footbridge take the middle of the three paths. This descends towards, and then crosses, Black Beck. An alternative is to cross the beck lower down and ascend on its far side. On the far side of the beck the path goes up to the small col (7) between Gale Fell and Melbreak. Follow this path until a fence with a gate is reached. Immediately before the gate turn right and go up the hillside for a short distance to another gate. Go through this and you are on the path (8) that leads through Mosedale to Loweswater.

At first this path can be very wet although not life-threateningly so. The area in the middle of the valley is very wet indeed and you are well advised to avoid it. The Mosedale path gradually improves and goes past the famous Mosedale Holly Tree (9) which has the unusual honour for a tree of a special mention on the OS map. A little further on the path joins another from the far side of the valley. It is then a clear, dry and fairly flat path all the way to Loweswater with Mosedale Beck meandering along on the left and Melbreak on the right.

After the exit from the valley the path becomes enclosed by stone walls with fields on either side (10). The first building on the left of the path as it gently descends to the village is a rather severe, grey, modern house with a functional, cylindrical chimney piercing its roof. This is followed by the rather-more-traditional Kirkgate Farm. The village is across the bridge over Park Beck and past the back of the Kirkstile Inn. In the centre is a small church dedicated to Saint Bartholomew (11). This was largely built in 1884 from an even smaller church which had been consecrated in 1829. The expansion was in anticipation of an increase in population as the result of a mine opening at the nearby Godferhead. In the event the mine failed and the population remained static. There are accounts of an even earlier chapel in the thirteenth or fourteenth century associated with St Bees Abbey. Before the seventeenth century there was a coffin route to St Bees via Carling Knott and Lamplugh although the actual track now seems obscure. For people starting at Loweswater there is (very) limited parking just over the bridge on the Mosedale side. One way the walk takes a little over two hours and is about eight kilometres long.

12) MOSES TROD (Wasdale Head Bridge)
(see also Sty Head Pass, Black Sale Pass, Burn Moor and circular walks 2, 5 and 11)

It is given to few of us to achieve immortality but Moses managed it. Who he was and why he used this path is disputed. Perhaps he was a quarryman called Moses Rigg who smuggled whisky or graphite. Another name for this route is 'Moses sledgegate' suggesting that slate was moved by sledge but sledges were generally used on downhill runs and Moses Trod is undulating to say the least and a harder calling would be difficult to imagine. Wainwright thought it unlikely that sledges were used, except on the downhill run to Honister, and favours packhorses. Whatever was used at least the whisky, if it were whisky, would have provided a bit of refreshment along the way.

Starting at the Honister end there is a car park (1) below the youth hostel and another in the slate works. Making your way through the depredations of the slate industry go up the steep, dismantled tramway (2) (marked as such on the OS map) to the ruined drum house (also marked) at its apex (3). This part of the tramway was a gravity system, a descending, loaded truck pulling up an unloaded one. About half way up was a crossing place with points said to be operated by a boy riding on the ascending truck. Past the drum house the truck was pulled by four horses to and from Dubs Quarry. It opened in 1891 and closed in 1932, the rails being removed during the Second World War. At the drum house go off to the left, pretty much at right angles, and head gently upwards along a cairned path (4) of variable visibility along the side of Grey Knotts and then Brandreth.

After walking for about twenty minutes the path goes between some rocks and turns to the left (5). Ignoring the cairned path here which leads

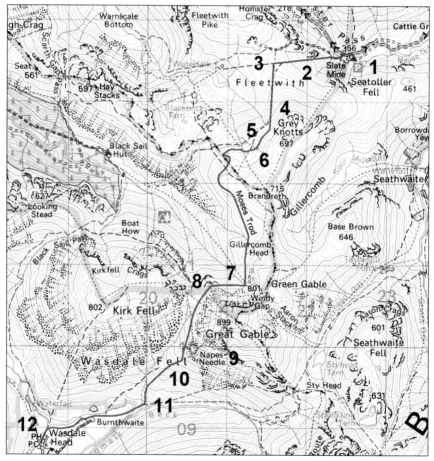

Map 20: Moses Trod.

off to the right, continue going uphill on the main path for another ten minutes or so towards an isolated and corroded iron fence post on top of a rock. Passing to the left of this, the summit of Great Gable comes into view straight ahead. Turn right here (6) towards a stile over a wire fence. This turn off is easily missed and, as is often the case, is easier to spot coming from the other direction. Go over the stile (there are three of them but any will do) and follow the path over the lip of the Ennerdale Valley.

Continue diagonally down the side of the Ennerdale Valley to cross its head at Stone Cove (7), some distance below the apex of the valley. The route then climbs fairly gently on a clear path below the rather forbidding rocks of the north face of Gable. Hidden somewhere up there are said to be the remains of a stone hut, known as the 'Smuggler's (i.e. Moses') Retreat'. According to Wainwright this is the highest site ever used for a building in England. The path heads towards the col between Gable and Kirk Fell but before reaching it skirts the side of Gable (8), well above Gable Beck, and only later starts its descent to Wasdale Head. Above and to the left are the White and Great Napes (9). The latter has the famous Napes Needle, the cradle of English rock climbing, first climbed by W. P. Haskett-Smith in 1886. Those wishing to emulate his achievement should ponder some of the headstones in the graveyard at Wasdale Head. For ordinary mortals it is probably better to watch performances on the Needle from the (relative) safety of the nearby 'Dress Circle'.

The path then descends along the wide ridge, called Gravel Neese (10),

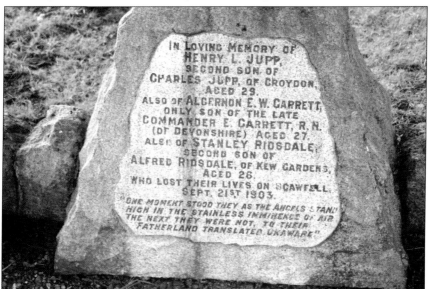

Plate 21: Gravestone in Wasdale Head graveyard.

almost to Lingmell Beck, and then turns right (11) to pass between eccen-
trically-shaped fields bordered by the dry stone walls that make this such
an attractive valley. The village (12) is little more than a kilometre further
on and has the Wasdale Head Inn, famous in climbing circles, as well as
an unmissable packhorse bridge. At least when Moses had reached here
the lake was not much further and the slate, if it were slate, could then be
moved by boat. The route is around eight kilometres and takes two to
three hours.

13) NAN BIELD PASS

(see also Garburn Pass, Gatesgarth Pass and circular walk 8)
Another path out of Mardale is over the delightful Nan Bield Pass.
Wainwright describes it as the finest of all the Lake District passes. The
path originally started at the centre of Mardale Green, or at least from outside the pub there, the Dun Bull. Now it starts near the car park at the
southern end of Haweswater (1). Take the middle of the three paths here.
It climbs gently and then more steeply with Small Water Beck to the right
until Small Water itself is reached. The beck is easily crossed (2) just
before the tarn and the path then passes close to the water's edge on its
north side.

There are three shelters here (3) built of slate which Wainwright
thought had been made for the convenience of travellers. If so they are
almost unique but Lake District weather being what it is perhaps he was
right and we should be grateful. The path climbs again after leaving the
tarn side but there are well thought out zigzags so the effort required, for
horse or walker, is not too great.

When the highest point of the pass is reached at about 640 metres (4)
there is a wonderful view of Kentmere and yet another shelter. The curious
name of the pass means the 'the mountain pass by Nan's shelter', Nan being
a shortened form of Anne, so some sort of shelter must have been here for
a long time. Who Nan (or Anne) was is unknown but the people here must
have been very considerate of travellers. The top of the pass is narrow with
mountain paths off to each side forming part of the Kentmere Round.

The way down to Kentmere is straight ahead, with zigzags leading
down to a gently descending path (5) alongside Kentmere Reservoir to the
hamlet of Overend (6). The reservoir was built in 1845/6 to control the
supply of water to the mills downstream on the River Kent. In the mid-
1990s it was emptied for repairs but has now been refilled. From Overend
the higher path leads to an old drove road (7) to Sadgill in Longsleddale,
which boasts a widened packhorse bridge. The lower path (8) goes to
Kentmere village (9) and from there another old drove road goes over

Garburn Pass to Troutbeck and then Ambleside. The Nan Bield path is about nine kilometres long and takes two and a half to three hours.

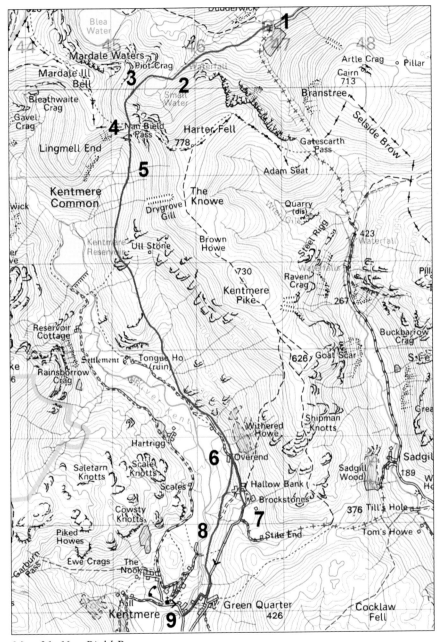

Map 21: Nan Bield Pass.
Reproduced by permission of Ordnance Survey on behalf of HMSO, © Crown copyright [2009]. All rights reserved. Ordnance Survey Licence number 100048757.

14) THE OLD COACH ROAD

The Old Coach Road is marked as such on the OS map and runs between Dockray in the Ullswater valley and St John's in the Vale near Keswick. It is certainly old but whether it was ever used by coaches is doubtful. Hindle considers it unlikely, and that the coaches went round by Scales and Troutbeck. He thinks it was a peat road, and for carts rather than coaches. Nevertheless it is pleasant to imagine a coach and horses speeding along it as one tramps its length and it is certainly flatter and wider than most of the other packhorse routes in the Lake District. The road is easy to walk and navigate and is about ten kilometres one way and takes around two and a half hours on foot. Although notices at both ends say that it is not suitable for motor vehicles it is certainly used by motor bikes and the parallel ruts suggest four wheels as well.

Starting at Dockray (1) there is parking for about five cars just on the Ullswater side of the bridge. There is considerably more parking a little way down the hill towards Ullswater to provide for visitors to Aira Force, a local beauty spot (and a packhorse bridge, see Aira Beck, page 23). Another option is to park at the end of the tarmac road out of Dockray where the wilder part of the Coach Road starts (3). This avoids about twenty minutes of road walking but may engender guilt feelings among those who feel they have to walk the entire route. Whelan offers two alternatives for the origin of the name Dockray, "the nook in a hollow" or "the

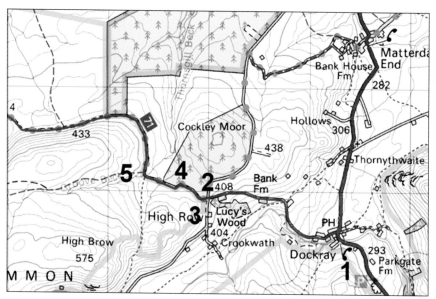

Map 22: The Old Coach road, east.

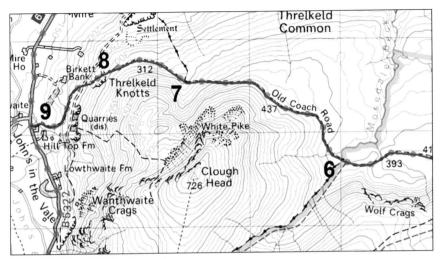

Map 23: The Old Coach road, west.

nook where dock or sorrel grows." It is a small hamlet with an hotel, on the road from Ullswater to Matterdale and Troutbeck.

Coming from the Ullswater direction, cross the bridge and turn left almost immediately. Walk slightly uphill past the front of the Royal Hotel keeping Aira Beck on the left. The houses and barn conversions are soon left behind as the road climbs further above and away from the beck. Follow the tarmac road for about a kilometre and a half until it turns abruptly to the right to form what is called the 'New Road' on the OS map (2). Do not go down this but go straight ahead for a few metres to the alternative car park (3). Ignore the road sign-posted to Dowthwaite and take the fork to the right, through a gate, and go along the wide track (4) with the plantation on Cockley Moor on the right. The track itself bears some signs of being maintained but has many puddles after rain.

Continue along this track and after a kilometre or so it turns to the right across a wooden footbridge alongside a nicely-engineered ford (5). Follow the track around, eventually passing Wolf Crags on the left. At this stage the path seems almost to be on a causeway between large boggy areas on each side. The track dips a little to cross Mosedale Beck (yet another Mosedale) by the unprepossessing Mariel Bridge (6).

Continue around Clough Head and descend gently with the re-entry between Clough Head and Thelkeld Knotts appearing on the left (7). Continue the descent to the far side of Thelkeld Knotts where spoil heaps appear on both sides of the path with a disused slate quarry on the left (8), presumably the source of the spoil. Although there is a profusion of tracks on the OS map most are old quarry tracks and the route of the 'Old Coach

Road' is obvious when you get there. Some woodland on the left disguises more spoil heaps. Spoil heaps take many years to become colonised by vegetation and become inconspicuous parts of the landscape, some never seem to, and perhaps areas of woodland like this, and the one on Garburn Pass, are better solutions to hiding them. Others would argue that quarries, mines and spoil heaps are part of the industrial history and topography of the Lake District and should not be hidden away. My own view is that they do not add much to the scenery.

The track then descends past a farm and the odd house to Wanthwaite (9) and the road (the B5322) between Thelkeld and Stanah that runs along Saint John's in the Vale. The Saint John relates to the Knights Hospitallers of the Order of Saint John who are thought to have had an establishment here in the thirteenth century, perhaps a hospice.

Unfortunately there is nothing in the way of refreshment here which might make the idea of starting at this end and lunching at the hotel in Dockray an attractive one. However parking is not easy, just one or two places along the road and at the entrance to the track. Perhaps the best option is to start at Dockray equipped with a packed lunch for Saint John's.

15) ORE GAP (Lingcove Bridge)
(see also Esk Hause and circular walks 4, 7 and 10)
This is one of the routes between Eskdale and Borrowdale, the other being via Esk Hause. Hindle thinks these passes were little used except possibly by the monks of Furness Abby to link their estates in Eskdale and Borrowdale. Ore Gap is one of the highest passes at 770 metres, slightly higher than Esk Hause at 759 metres. The route is shared with that to Esk Hause until Lingcove Bridge is reached.

Starting from the informal car park on the grassy area beside the road at the foot of the Hardknott Pass in Eskdale (1), go along the road towards the pass. After a short distance turn left by the telephone kiosk and go along the road (2) towards Brotherikeld farm. This unusual name may owe something to the brothers of Furness Abbey but it has an even earlier origin. The 'brother' part comes from the Old Norse for booths or huts and the second part from the name of an individual - Ulfkell; hence "Ulfkell's booths or huts." The farm was purchased by the National Trust in 1961 to prevent afforestation of the land hereabouts. The path goes to the left of the farm, staying close to the River Esk. It continues along the valley (3), never straying far from the river, until the Esk is joined by Lingcove Beck. This is the site of Lingcove Bridge (4), well worth a photograph or two.

The route to Ore Gap passes to the right of the bridge and goes straight on, keeping Lingcove Beck to the left and climbs up some soggy grassland

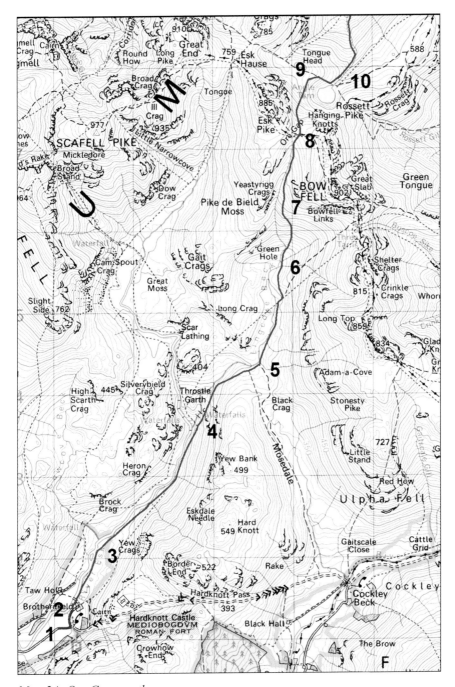

Map 24: Ore Gap, south.
Reproduced by permission of Ordnance Survey on behalf of HMSO, © Crown copyright
[2009]. All rights reserved. Ordnance Survey Licence number 100048757.

to follow the beck around and into a pleasant valley (5). The path becomes less distinct but roughly follows the river on the left with Crinkle Crags followed by Bowfell in the distance on the right. It continues to go north along the valley floor (6) and then climbs (7) fairly steeply between

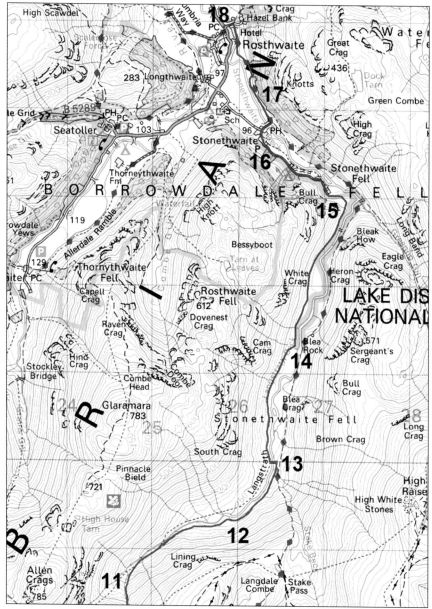

Map 25: Ore Gap, north.

Bowfell and Esk Pike. At the top is Ore Gap (8). No doubt the name refers to iron ore but whether it was mined there, or the miners or the ore just passed through it, is uncertain. There is a path down the far side to the thoroughfare (9) between the Langdale Valley and Sty Head Pass. Angle Tarn is on the right.

Hindle shows a route close to Allencraggs Gill descending into Langstrath, as does the OS map, but I have been unable to find it and if it did exist it would have involved a steep descent into the Langstrath Valley. My feeling is the the route would have gone down to the path just before the outlet from Angle Tarn and then (10) followed Angletarn Gill down to Langstrath. Whichever is correct they both meet at the junction of Allencraggs Gill and Angletarn Gill at the foot of the steep end to the Langstrath Valley (11). There is a clear path to the right of the river (12) and then paths on both sides all the way to Stonethwaite. If you wish you can cross the river by the foot bridge where another path comes down from Stake Pass (13). After Blackmoss Pot (14) the path on the left side is wider and flatter.

The iron ore was smelted at a bloomery on Smithymire Island (15) at the mouth of the valley where Greenup Gill meets Langstrath Beck to form Stonethwaite Beck. Smithy refers to smelting metals and mire means a bog or swamp. Langstrath means a long valley with marshy ground overgrown with brushwood. It requires about five tons of wood to produce one ton of charcoal and three tons of charcoal to produce one ton of iron so it is easy to see that the trees would have disappeared fairly quickly. The reason for the bloomery being sited on an island was to use the surrounding water to drive hammers to convert the crude iron into wrought iron. The 'bloom' was a mixture of iron, charcoal and various other impurities extracted from the bottom of the furnace.

Rosthwaite (18) is about a kilometre and a half down the road from Stonethwaite (16) or more pleasantly along the path (17) on the far side of the river, now part of the Cumbria Way. One way is getting on for twenty kilometres and takes six or seven hours.

16) ROSSETT GILL PASS (Wasdale Head Bridge)
(see also Stake Pass, Sty Head Pass, Ore Gap and circular walks 5, 6 and 7)
The Wasdale to Ambleside route was one of the most important in packhorse times, taking traffic from the west coast to the centre of the Lake District and beyond. The route went from Wasdale Head to Sty Head, along the well-worn path to the head of the Langdale Valley via Rossett Gill Pass and then along the floor of the valley, ultimately to Ambleside. It seems pointless to trudge along roads all the way to or from Ambleside

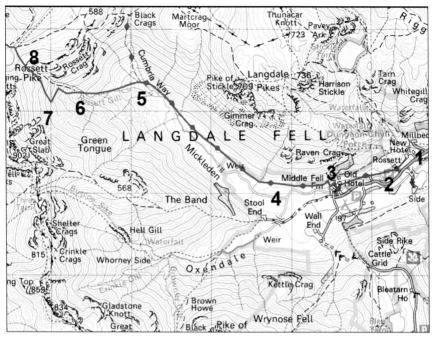

Map 26: Rossett Gill, east.

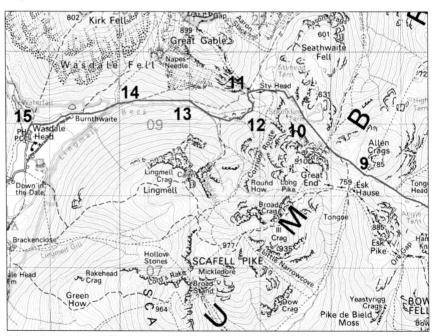

Map 27: Rossett Gill, west.

and I have chosen the car park near the Old Dungeon Gill Hotel as the best starting place. If this is full there is a larger one near the New Dungeon Gill Hotel. The walk takes four to five hours in one direction from the Old Hotel and about another fifteen minutes from the New. This makes it a long day for going both ways and it might be better to turn around some-where on the top path between Rossett Gill Pass and Sty Head or do a round trip via Stake Pass (see Circular Walk 7, page 149).

If you have started at the New Hotel (1), there are three ways of reach-ing the Old Hotel. Two paths leave towards the bottom of the car park next to the Stickle Barn. The higher one goes along the side of the valley as far as the Old Hotel. It drops down a little just beyond and behind the hotel to join the wide valley-floor path. The lower path (2), which is less effort and might be the best choice, goes through fields and across a small wooden bridge to reach the road in front of the Old Hotel (3). Not long after leaving the car park this path goes in front of a house called 'Rossett'. Rossett prob-ably comes from old Norse and means a horse pasture. This seventeenth century property was used to rest and shelter the packhorses which had come over Rossett Gill and Stake Passes and is believed to have given its name to the gill. The third alternative is to go along the tarmac road on the valley floor, or perhaps you should save that for when you are coming back.

Starting at the Old Hotel car park (3), go behind the hotel to find the wide path. Walk first west and then north west along the flat valley floor path (4) with Mickledon Beck on the left and mountains rising steeply on both sides. This is a classic, glaciated, U-shaped valley and although it car-ries a heavy traffic of walkers, particularly in the summer, it is so large that it never feels crowded. After about three kilometres the path divides (5) with the right hand fork zigzagging up to Stake Pass while the left heads towards Rossett Gill. The direct route up the gill is heavily eroded and something of a trial and is not recommended. A better choice is to follow the excellent made-up path (6) that zigzags to the left of the gill. This is always clear and easy to follow. The pass rises to about 610 metres although it feels higher and steeper than it really is. Perhaps this is because all the climb is at the end of the valley and is in one continuous stretch.

The last zig (or zag) of this path goes out further than the others and goes above some big slabs of rock with water running over them. At the furthest point of this deviation, where the path forms an acute angle (7), it is possible to make out another path moving off to the south. This is the old packhorse route. It is difficult to see now as its traffic has been taken by the path already described but it continued over the wet slabs and zig-zagged down the side of Green Tongue. It then crossed a dry gully about two thirds of the way down and shortly afterwards contoured along the lower part of Green Tongue to reach Mickleden Beck just before Grunting Gill. Parts of the route can be seen in the distance when coming down from Stake Pass, particularly where it crosses the gully. It is well described by Wainwright but is now difficult to follow and is not shown on the OS map. Although I am entirely in favour of following historical routes I think on this occasion, reluctantly, the conventional route is the better choice. Wainwright also mentions "The Packwoman's grave", although he is coy about its exact location, and a hidden sheepfold, both of which remained hidden from me.

Over the top of the pass (8), the clear path dips down to Angle Tarn and then climbs steadily to the col (9) between Esk Hause and Allen Crags. This is the highest point of the walk at over 620 metres. The path then descends as it goes towards Great Gable, passing Sprinkling Tarn on the right (10). As it comes down from the tarn the path curves to the left and joins the route across Sty Head Pass (11). There are several paths here but the packhorse route (12) to Wasdale zigzags down to cross Spouthead Gill and is shown on the OS map. The beginning of the route is some 50 metres past the stretcher box towards Wasdale. It is not obvious, although there is a small cairn, and it starts by descending along a grassy, v-shaped hollow. It becomes clearer lower down and provides a pleasant alternative to the more direct, but rocky, walkers' route which moves along the southern flank of Gable.

The path descends quite quickly and crosses what becomes Lingmell Gill to join another of the paths coming down from Sty Head a little further down (13). This path then descends gently towards Wasdale Head joining the main walkers' path from Sty Head and Moses Trod just before the fields start (14). These fields are famous for their unusual shapes and the delightful pictures made by the shadows from their dry stone walls but they are best seen from the mountain tops. The path crosses a long wooden bridge, with a supporting pier, over Gable Beck and then goes over several small bridges. Wasdale Head (15) has an hotel, a shop, several farms, a church and, of course, a superb bridge. If you start at this end there is ample parking on the village green, a short distance along the road towards the lake. The walk is about fourteen kilometres in one direction.

17) SCANDALE PASS (High Sweden Bridge and possibly Hartsop Bridge) *(see also High Sweden bridge, short walk 3 and circular walk 3)*
Scandale was an alternative route to the better known Kirkstone Pass but was less used because it is some 100 metres higher. This no doubt accounts for why the inn was built on Kirkstone and not Scandale. Kirkstone is now an unattractive route for the walker with streams of cars straining up each

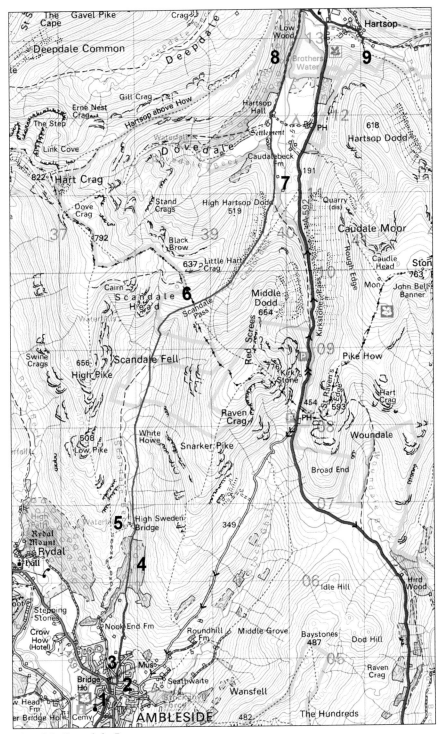

Map 28: Scandale Pass.
© Crown Copyright and/or database right. All rights reserved. Licence number 100048757.

side but it can be seen from various parts of this path and its history appreciated as an important packhorse route. At the northern end of Kirkstone there are still some signs of the Roman road which went over the pass. Most of it is now covered by tarmac but it can be seen as it diverges from the A592 to cross Kirkstone Beck at NY403092. It eventually joins the Scandale route in the valley bottom but is largely invisible from the walk. Not long after the start High Sweden Bridge can be admired. At the Brothers Water end of the route a short extension can be made to Hartsop with its bridge but perhaps the walk is long enough already and Hartsop can wait for another day.

The route starts in the centre of Ambleside (1) and goes along the main road towards Rydal, passing Bridge House on the left, and then turns right just before the Armitt Museum to go up the road (2) towards the Kirkstone Pass. Shortly after the Golden Rule pub it turns left onto Kirkstone Road and then quickly left again onto Sweden Bridge Lane. At the end of the tarmac road (3) it goes through a gate leading to a continuously rising rough track with stone walls on each side. Soon there is a pleasing view to the left towards Rydal with the Langdales in the distance. Beyond this the path becomes flatter and enters woodland with a stream on the left in a small ravine. The path goes over the spoil heaps (4) from two disused slate quarries on the right. Not long afterwards High Sweden Bridge (5) comes into view on the left.

The packhorse route passes to the right of the bridge a few yards before it is reached so the bridge must just have been used for access to the fields beyond or for another track up from Ambleside via Nook End and Low Sweden Bridge. The route continues north along the obvious path towards Scandale Pass which becomes visible in the distance. In due course the path becomes less enclosed. There is a high corrie (even a small hanging valley) visible to the left on the side of the hills making up the first limb of the Fairfield Horseshoe, happily tramped by thousands every year. At the end of the valley there are zigzags going up to the summit of the pass (6) at about 520 metres. On the far side of the pass the path is less distinct and moves a little to the right. Just down from the summit, the top (southwest) end of Ullswater becomes visible and the lower part of Kirkstone Pass can be seen in the distance on the right. The descent is on a rocky path with the stream to the right as Brothers Water becomes visible in the distance ahead. The path continues to descend until it reaches the valley floor (7) and ultimately Brothers Water itself (8). The name is thought to refer to two brothers who were drowned while skating on it in 1785. It is also one of the few lakes where a rare fish called the schelly lives.

There is another bridge a little further on at Hartsop (9) although its connection with the Scandale Pass route is tenuous. If you want to see this bridge go along the motor road towards Kirkstone and then turn left and walk along the narrow road towards Hartsop village. Follow the road through the delightful village and the car park and the bridge is at the beginning of the path that leads to (the unfortunately named) Pasture Bottom. Then you have to walk back. Both ways adds up to about 22 kilometres taking six hours or so.

18) SCARTH GAP
(see also Black Sail Pass and circular walks 1 and 2)
Scarth Gap is the pass between the Buttermere valley and Ennerdale. Scarth means a notch or gap as did pass originally. However 'pass' came to refer to tracks running through gaps, in this case a packhorse route, hence "the gap through which packhorses go."

This route probably started at Buttermere village but starts and finishes are often arbitrary and to avoid walking on the road a closer start is at the farm at Gatesgarth (1) at the foot of the western end of Honister Pass. There is a convenient car park here. Alternatively start at Buttermere

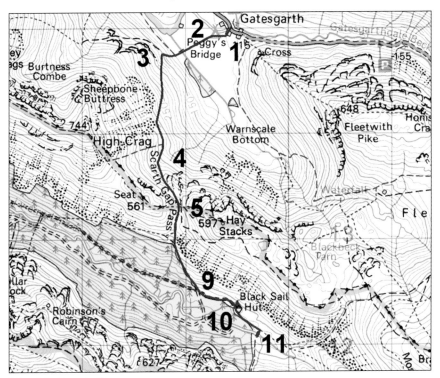

Map 29: Scarth Gap.

(village) and take the lakeside path that goes through Wilkinsyke Farm. It does involve a short stretch on the road closer to Gatesgarth but the views over the lake make it all worthwhile, and you get to go through a tunnel. There is parking in Buttermere.

At Gatesgarth cross the road from the car park to the path that runs alongside the farm yard and then goes between the fields (2) that lie to the south east of Buttermere. The path is completely flat until the far side of Buttermere is reached. It then diverts to the right and then to the left (3) and climbs fairly steadily (4) and in several sections towards Scarth Gap. There is a quicker, but much steeper, path that misses out the first zigzag.

At first the path is obvious but it becomes less clear and more stony the higher it gets. There is another path that forks off to the right about two thirds of the way up and climbs steeply towards High Crag but our route climbs more gently to the col between Hay Stacks on the left and Seat on the right. The apex (5) is at about 400 metres. When achieved it rewards the walker with impressive views of the far side of the Ennerdale Valley with the magnificent Pillar Rock (6) to the right and Kirk Fell (7) and then Great Gable (8) to the left. The path then becomes indistinct but the route goes straight ahead and then down (9) to the valley floor alongside an area of harvested forest.

At the bottom it turns left and goes on the wide track past the Black Sail Hut (10), the Mecca of English youth hosteling. Rather like Skiddaw House (q.v.) and Mosedale Cottage (q.v.) all who stay here have had to walk or cycle as there is no vehicular access, at least for visitors. A little way beyond the hut the path turns to the right and goes down to and then crosses the stream (11) and the steepish ascent to the Black Sail Pass starts. If you continue on over Black Sail you have a fair walk back with four sections of climb. On the other hand you can look at the exquisite bridge at Wasdale Head. Just doing Scarth Gap from Gatesgarth takes around one and half hours and covers about four kilometres.

19) SKIDDAW

The area east of Skiddaw is open and empty and quite unlike most of the Lake District. It is variously referred to as Back o'Skidda or Skiddaw Forest. Forest in this context means a medieval hunting ground rather than an area of trees. The packhorse route passes between Thelkeld, just off the road between Penrith and Keswick, and the village of Bassenthwaite. According to Whelan there are various explanations for the derivation of the word Skiddaw, none of which seems totally convincing. Thelkeld means "the thralls' (i.e. slaves') spring." There are several springs nearby but the slaves have gone.

Starting at Thelkeld (1), there is a car park in the village centre and another just up the road towards the Blencathra Centre sign-posted 'Blease Road, leads to Blencathra.' This road goes past the school and the Mission Hall and then between fields up the hill side for about two kilometres and ends at the Blencathra Centre where there is another car park (2). Unless you feel the need to walk along the road this would seem the most sensible car park to chose. The path leaves this car park at its far end and would be hard to miss. It is wide and in good condition and moves around the

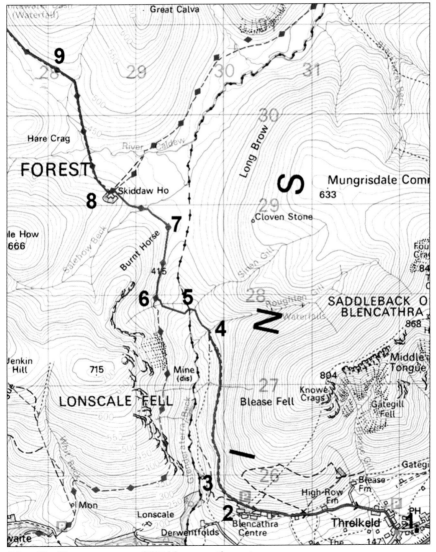

Map 30: The route east of Skiddaw, south part.

side (3) of Blease Fell some distance above Glenderaterra Beck. Apart
from the Glen part, meaning valley, the derivation of this curious, and difficult to pronounce, name seems obscure. On the far side of the valley is
the path from Keswick that now forms part of the Cumbria Way. This is a
113 kilometre walk from Ulverston to Carlisle and goes along part of the
packhorse route a little further on.

   On the far side of the valley, below the Cumbria Way, are the tell-tale
spoil heaps below a disused mine. The path goes past a small re-entry with
a waterfall and about half a kilometre further on crosses a more substantial stream on a small, but wide, double clapper bridge (4). This is really
not much more than a few stones placed over two water channels and
some might consider the title of 'bridge' to be a little presumptuous, but it
keeps your feet dry. The path then descends towards the river in the valley
bottom (5). There is a sheep fold on the left and then two wooden foot
bridges, one of which is a simply supported beam and the other a beam
fixed at each end.

   Over the river the path climbs the far side of the valley to join the
Cumbria Way (6). It then continues around the end of Burnt Horse (7). This
route seems to have a plethora of strange names. The 'horse' here means a
neck of land rather than the animal and the burning may have been deliber-
ate to encourage new growth. As the corner is turned a clump of trees with
a substantial house (8) in its midst becomes visible in the distance. This is
Skiddaw House and is one of the most remote houses in the Lake District. It
was built in about 1829 by the Earl of Egremont as a base for grouse shooting and for the keepers who managed the estate. It was later divided into two
houses, one for a shepherd and the other for a gamekeeper.   The last

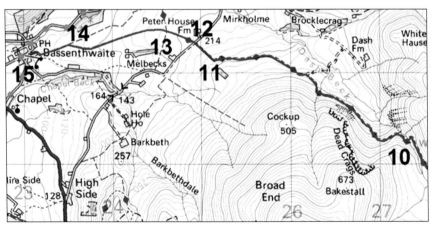

Map 31: The route east of Skiddaw, north part.

shepherd departed in 1969 and the building stayed empty until 1991 when it became a Youth Hostel. This subsequently closed but is now (2007) open again in the summer as a bunkhouse for about 20 people. It was the setting of a murder in one of Hugh Walpole's *Rogue Herries* series. The house has spectacular views down big valleys in front and behind. Further behind is the massive bulk of Skiddaw itself, the fourth highest mountain in England at 931 metres. The path goes just in front of the grounds of the house and continues straight ahead. One branch of the Cumbria Way continues along the same path but the other moves off at right angles along the side of the Caldew Valley to Latrigg.

The route continues in a roughly north west direction slowly descending to cross a small stream by a ford and a footbridge and then climbing, but not by much, to cross the pass (9) between Great Calva on the right and Bakestall on the left. Over the pass the route descends along the side of Little Calva. Calva probably means the 'hill where calves graze.' The path then doubles back in a descending zigzag and crosses (10) Whitewater Dash, a waterfall, on a delightful little arched bridge. It has no parapets and the arch is below road level so there is no hump. The waterfall is below the bridge and a better view of it is obtained a little further down. The path skirts around Bakestall, almost as far as Cockup. This is not a comment on the navigational skills of local walkers but possibly means the "blind valley frequented by wild birds."

The route then joins a narrow tarmac road (11) that goes between fields until it meets the wider road at Peter House Farm (12). From here the route degenerates into, at best, a muddy path that goes from field to field until it reaches Bassenthwaite village. Unless you are determined to see Bassenthwaite it might be as well to stop here and turn around. Alternatively if you start at the Bassenthwaite end there is a small car park here at the side of the road.

If you do decide to walk to Bassenthwaite go across the road and into the field opposite. Rather than following a farm track leading straight across the field, go diagonally to the left to leave the field by a stile near to an electricity pole. At the sign post on the far side of the stile the Cumbria Way parts company (13) and goes off to the right to Orthwaite. Continue on at the side of the next few fields looking for the white poles that indicate the stiles or gates. Closer to the village the path turns to the right to move diagonally across a field (14); again a white pole indicates the route. It is then just a short walk to the village (15).

Bassenthwaite is about a kilometre and a half from the lake of the same name. It has two pubs, two churches, a chapel and limited parking. If you chose to start here you should leave the village green by Back Hill where there is a sign post to Peter House Farm. Follow the posts as described above and cross the tarmac road at Peter House Farm to enter the narrow road on the opposite side. Continue on this for a little more than a kilometre and then branch off to the right at a sign on a rock saying 'Skiddaw House, Thelkeld (and) Dash Falls.' The path ahead is clear all the way to Thelkeld. The walk is a little over fourteen kilometres and takes about three and a half hours in one direction.

20) STAKE PASS
(see also Rossett Gill Pass and circular walks 6 and 7)
This route connects the top of the Langdale Valley with Borrowdale via Langstrath. Langdale is a long wide valley much frequented by walkers and climbers and was an important packhorse route running west to east in the middle of the Lake District.

To get to the pass use the car park next to the Old Dungeon Ghyll Hotel and join the path just behind the hotel that goes along the valley floor. As this is a popular spot there is a fair chance that this car park will be full. In that case there are more places in the car park (1) near to the Stickle Barn which in turn is next to the New Dungeon Ghyll Hotel. This means a short walk along the road or along one of the paths on the north side of the valley (2) (see Rossett Gill Pass, page 89). From the Old Hotel (3) the path is wide and obvious (4) and pretty well flat until it reaches the notorious Rossett Gill at the far end. Notorious because the direct route up is very eroded and well worth avoiding (but see below and Rossett Gill Pass).

Stake Pass is to the right (5) just before Rossett Gill is reached. The route upwards is obvious and along a series of well-engineered zigzags. The top of the pass (6) is wide but relatively dry and takes about half an hour to cross. Then follows a pleasant zigzagging descent (7), with Stake Beck on the right, down to Langstrath (8), another long valley. Turning right and going over a wooden bridge the path (9) follows Langstrath Beck and eventually leads to Stonethwaite and then onto Rosthwaite on part of the Cumbria Way.

An alternative route at the bottom of the pass is to cross the other footbridge to the far side of Langstrath Beck and walk along the less-undulating path (10) on that side of the river. It becomes much wider after Blackmoss Pot (11). Just after Stonethwaite (12) there is another bridge, over Stonethwaite Beck, to reach the pleasant path mentioned above (13) to Rosthwaite (14).

Langstrath is a long valley and a shorter walk would be to turn back at the Langstrath end of Stake Pass and retrace your steps back up the pass or, slightly longer, turn left and go up Langstrath and then come back

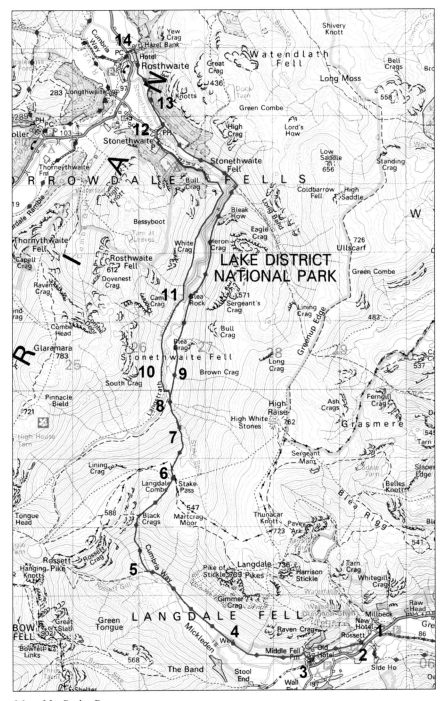

Map 32: Stake Pass.

down Rossett Gill. I know I said it was very eroded and best avoided but there is an alternative path just to the south of the eroded track. At the top this was the start of the old packhorse route but the excellent made-up path deviates from the historic route after the first zig and turns back towards the gill. An even shorter alternative is to turn left at the top of Stake Pass, follow the ridge path to Rossett Pike and then go down Rossett Gill and head back along the Langdale Valley for tea. The walk all the way to Rosthwaite is about thirteen kilometres and takes three to four hours.

21) STICKS PASS

Sticks Pass long ago lost the original sticks that marked its route although some, presumably replacements, were reported by Barber and Atkinson in 1928. None remain now. It leads from Stanah, at the north end of Thirlmere where it joined the route from Grasmere to Keswick, over the col between Stybarrow Dodd and Raise down to Glenridding and Ullswater. As the route from Grasmere to Ullswater would have been easier via Grisedale the traffic must have been mainly to and from Keswick.

At the Thirlmere end the route starts by a signpost to the right of the road to St. Johns in the Vale (1), just after it leaves the main road from Grasmere to Keswick. There is some parking just off the road and more in the grounds of the parish hall. The route starts up the short tarmac road by the parish hall and then goes over a stile and shortly afterwards crosses an open aqueduct (2) that flows towards Thirlmere. This is Thirlmere Leat or Water Race. It was constructed to collect water from several becks that ran

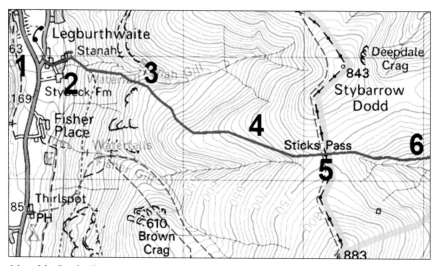

Map 33: Sticks Pass, west.

down from the Helvellyn range which had hitherto not reached the newly enlarged Thirlmere reservoir (see Watendlath). It reaches the reservoir at NY313169 via a tunnel under the A591.

The path continues up a steep set of zigzags (3) with Stanah Gill on the left in a deepening ravine. At the top of this slope on the right are the stony ruins of a building. The clear path continues along the side (4) of Stybarrow Dodd with Sticks Gill in a V-shaped valley on the right. Curiously the gill on the far side of the pass has the same name. Eventually the path reaches the watershed at 738 metres where there is a tumbledown cairn (5). The path that crosses at right angles along the broad ridge is exceptionally wide and clear. According to Hindle this was the next highest pass in general use after Esk Hause. It was probably first used in the late seventeenth century for carrying ore from Greenside mine, further down the valley towards Glenridding, to a smelter at Keswick.

The route descends along a rather eroded path (6) with (the other) Sticks Gill on the right. It then curves to the right below an area of land slip high up on the left (7) caused by the collapse of the workings beneath it. The path continues past the remains of a dam and various water channels and then over a wooden foot bridge (8). There are several spoil heaps around here and a ruined building on the left. Ullswater becomes visible at about this point. The path descends, curves around Stang End and zigzags down steeply (9), partly on more spoil and a tailings dam. Tailings are the waste materials left behind after the best ore has been extracted and are a mixture of depleted ore and any chemicals used in the extraction process

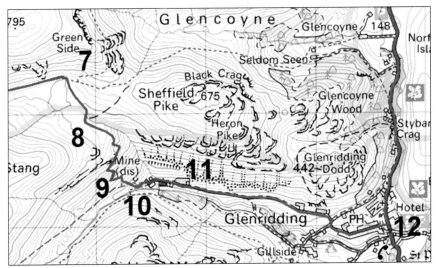

Map 34: Sticks Pass, east.

and are often very toxic. As Greenside was principally a lead mine (there was some silver extraction as well) the tailings here are heavily contaminated and pose something of a risk should they escape en masse and descend into Ullswater. Directly below is a leat which would have been used to carry water for the extraction processes. On the 28 October 1927 Kepple Lower Dam, in the adjacent valley, burst after a period of heavy rainfall and a quarter of a million gallons of water careered through a gap 30 metres wide and ten metres deep to reach Glenridding Village shortly afterwards. Amazingly nobody was killed although several people had narrow escapes. Below and to the left is yet another enormous tailings dam (10) which has been partly grassed over. A little below the leat the path flattens out and passes between several nicely-restored buildings that no doubt were originally part of the mine. The mine itself started in about 1690 and closed in 1962. It was the largest in the Lake District and has very extensive underground workings. In 1892 it boasted the first electric locomotive used in a British mine.

The route crosses Swart Beck on a bridge and gently descends to Glenridding on the economically-concreted Greenside Road (11). On the left is the old explosives store for the mine, tactfully sited some distance away from the other buildings. Although this is a mine road it was probably built on the the old packhorse route as it is the best way down to Glenridding. The route passes the Travellers Rest pub on the left and ends in the large car park at Glenridding (12). It is just over eight kilometres and takes about three hours one way. Walking it the other way around is less steep, at least to start with. Hardier souls will not mind as they will just do it both ways.

22) STY HEAD PASS (Stockley and Wasdale Head bridges)
(see also Burn Moor, Moses Trod and circular walks 5 and 11)
Sty Head means "the top of the pass" (Whaley). In ancient times it was called Edderlanghals which could be taken to mean "the long pass by the rapidly flowing stream" (Readyhough). Either seems appropriate. It was an important packhorse route connecting Wasdale and the west coast with Borrowdale and was engineered for much of its length. It had a narrow escape from the road makers in the late nineteenth and early twentieth centuries. It is now a path much used by fell walkers making their way to the Scafell Range and Great Gable.

There is parking at either end but I have chosen to start at Seathwaite (1) with its ample parking on the verge leading up to the farm. Go through the farm and continue on the clear stony path beyond (2). The wide and stony river bed on the right serves as a reminder that this is the wettest inhabited place in England with an annual rainfall of about 3.3 metres. Continue along this path, with the River Derwent on the right, for about a kilometre. Cross over the widened and rebuilt Stockley Bridge (3) and go straight ahead. The path to the left goes up Ruddy Gorge and can be saved for another day.

The path goes up over some rocky bits (4) but then curves around well above the water falls of Taylorgill Force and then climbs more gently alongside Styhead Gill ultimately crossing it on a wooden foot bridge (5). The path continues in a south-westerly direction on almost flat ground and passes Styhead Tarn on the left (6). It then climbs a little to the highest point of the pass at 488 metres (7). Several routes meet in this area, three of them leading to Wasdale. The packhorse route is the one on the left with the most southerly direction (8). It is a little difficult to find at first although there is a small cairn on the left about 50 metres beyond the stretcher box leading to a grassy, v-shaped hollow that the path goes down. It becomes more obvious as it descends on a series of pleasant zigzags and crosses Spouthead Gill. It then sweeps around, descending all the time, crossing Lingmell Beck to join one of the other paths about 500 metres further on (9).

On the left is the infamous ravine containing Piers Gill (10). In the

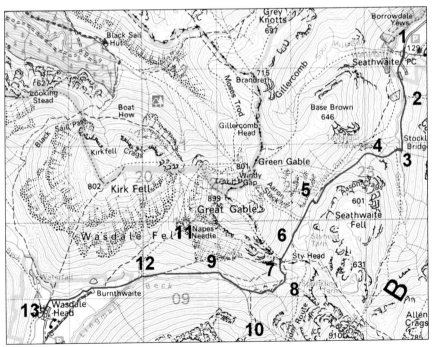

Map 35: Sty Head Pass.

early 1900s a climber fell here and broke both ankles. He lay there for eighteen days, fortunately beside some water, before being rescued. On the right, Napes Needle (11) can just be made out high up on the side of Gable. This still provides a challenge to rock climbers although modern equipment and techniques have made it more accessible. The path continues along the right bank of Lingmell Beck and eventually joins the higher, and more frequented, walkers' path from Sty Head. Shortly afterwards it is also joined by Moses Trod (12) over from Honister. Soon the path goes between the delightful fields of Wasdale Head with their evocative stone walls and over several small streams with little wooden bridges. The village itself (13) is about a kilometre further on. One way is about eight kilometres and takes between two and a half and three hours.

23) WALNA SCAR ROAD (Walna Scar Bridge)

The derivation of Walna is obscure but scar means an escarpment. This route, or road as it is here, was mainly for carrying slate from the local quarries but was used by other traffic as well. It stretches west from Coniston, a small town heavily linked in the past to mining, to Seathwaite in the Duddon Valley. Coniston means "The King's estate or village", possibly some small Norse kingdom, now long forgotten.

Starting at the Coniston end there is a large car park (1) in the town centre and some street parking as well. From the car park turn left, go past the

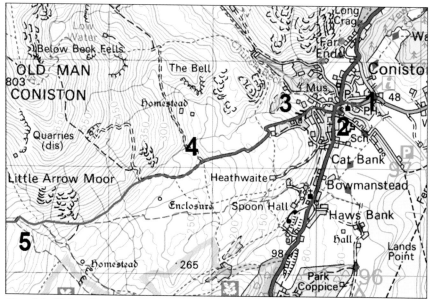

Map 36: Walna Scar Road, east.

church, turn left onto the main road and go over the bridge. Shortly afterwards turn right to go up Station Road (2) which heads away from the lake
and towards the fells. This bends to the left and goes up a steep tarmac
road (3) sign-posted 'Walna Scar Coniston Old Man.' On the left, just
before this bend, there is another car park on Old Furness Road. Follow
the Walna Scar Road and eventually it reaches the open fells. This is a hard
start because it is so steep so early in the walk. It is possible to avoid it
completely by taking your car up here as there is yet another car park (4)
at the end of the tarmac road but the road is narrow as well as steep and
has few passing places.

   After the last car park the route becomes rocky and wet in places but is
perfectly clear and easy to walk. There is a sign saying motor vehicles are
not supposed to go any further than the car park but judging by the tyre
marks they certainly do. The path skirts around the foot of Coniston Old
Man on the right. Later on there is a path to the Old Man clearly marked
with a painted sign on a rock. Above is a slate quarry which appears still
active (2007), unlike the many others which have left their scars and spoil
heaps on the mountain sides around here. In the distance to the left are several large windmills. Behind, Coniston Water has emerged from the trees.

   The path continues and passes the entrance to the cove leading to Goats
Water. The Walna Scar Bridge (5) is here, over one of the streams from
Goats Water. Iron hand rails have been added but it is otherwise fairly intact

Plate 22: Walna Scar Bridge.

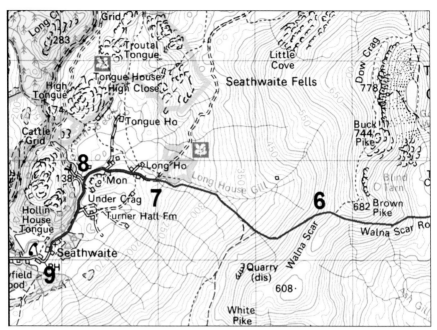

Map 37: Walna Scar Road, west.

although the top of the arch on the downstream side is a little flattened. The path then zigzags steeply to the summit of Walna Scar (6) with some disused quarries on the right and the remains of a slate building. Perhaps they were the ones for which the road was built but there are quarries and mines all over the Coniston fells. Just before the summit of the pass there is a small slate shelter, rather like the ones on the way to Nan Bield. On the top a whole new world opens out with Sca Fell and Scafell Pike in the distance to the north and Sellafield and the sea to the west beyond the Duddon Valley. On a clear day the mountains of the Isle of Man can be seen on the horizon.

The route descends fairly steeply on a good path with a wide zigzag. There are several spoil heaps from disused quarries lower down on the left and some ruined buildings. Eventually the path goes through a gate and its surface becomes more rocky as it descends less steeply with Long House Gill on the right (7). The valley bottom is reached and with it a tarmac road which goes to the right of a white-painted house. This narrow road curves round the back of Hollin House Haw (8) and joins the main valley road to Seathwaite (9) which is about a kilometre down the road.

Starting at the Seathwaite end there is only limited parking. There is even a sign near the pub saying 'Do not park and walk' which is

understandable but reflects the lack of an alternative. There is very limited parking just across the road from the church and a little way towards
the pass. The parish room has some space around it but nothing to say that
you can park there. Perhaps an honesty box would help them raise money
to cure the damp problem mentioned on their notice board. One way the
walk is about nine kilometres and takes around two and a half hours.

24) WATENDLATH (Watendlath Bridge)
(see also short walk 10 and circular walk 12)
This route crosses between Wythburn at the southern end of Thirlmere and
Rosthwaite in the Borrowdale Valley. It links the thoroughfare between
Grasmere and Keswick that now carries so much motor traffic with the
more peaceful Borrowdale Valley via the pretty hamlet of Watendlath.
This is a delightful if rather long and at times wet walk at about seventeen
kilometres if you go there and back. It entails four separate climbs, which
should be enough for anyone, and takes about four hours in each direction.
There is ample parking at either end in official car parks. At the Thirlmere
end the best car park is just to the north of Dob Gill Bridge on the road that
passes along the west side of Thirlmere. Enthusiasts may want to start at
Wythburn but this involves a stretch on the road and is hardly worth the
effort, although it does go past a nice farm. At Rosthwaite there is a car
park on the side road that leaves the centre of the village heading west for
the River Derwent and another next to the Scafell Hotel.

Thirlmere, or "the lake with the narrowing" was much enlarged by
Manchester Corporation building a dam at its outlet in the late nineteenth
century. It did, indeed, have a 'narrowing', in fact it was almost divided
into two by the promontory of Armboth and the land below Dalehead Hall.
The village of Armboth disappeared into the rising waters and not much
remains of Wythburn apart from the church. Only one of the twelve farms
in Wythburn and Armboth listed in the 1851 census remains. There was
considerable local opposition but the bill to construct the dam and the
other works passed easily at the second attempt in 1879. Thirlmere has
remained much as it was after the reservoir was formed as Manchester
bought most of the surrounding land. It has a rather sterile appearance with
the wide shore line characteristic of reservoirs. On the other hand there are
few buildings and few people to disturb the peace. Recently many of the
lakeside trees have been felled leading to a rather devastated appearance
in places.

The aqueduct to Manchester is 154 kilometres long and the water runs
along it at six kilometres per hour, entirely by gravity, and takes just over
a day to reach its destination. Curiously there is a group of people (the

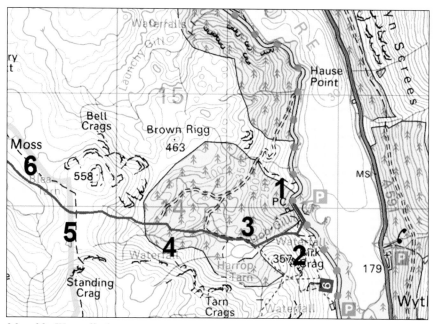

Map 38: Watendlath, east

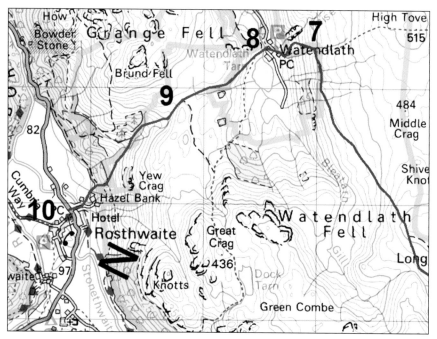

Map 39: Watendlath, west.
Reproduced by permission of Ordnance Survey on behalf of HMSO, © Crown copyright
[2009]. All rights reserved. Ordnance Survey Licence number 100048757.

'Nutters Mobile Surveillance Unit') who spend their leisure time plotting the positions of access gates along the course of the aqueduct. In case you are tempted to join them there is a walking guide to the 210 kilometres of the Thirlmere Way written by Tim Cappelli. The aqueduct from Haweswater takes an entirely different route although there are links.

Starting at the Wythburn end, leave the Dob Gill car park (1) and head south towards Wythburn and go along the road and over the bridge. Turn right almost immediately after the bridge at a signpost to Watendlath. Go up a steep and rocky path (2) with Dob Gill on the right. Unlike a good child, this is heard rather than seen as you ascend. More or less at the top, the path turns to the right and goes over a wall to enter pleasant woodland. This is largely, but not entirely, made up of conifers. Some of the trees are impressively large and have some breathing space around them. The whole thing is a welcome change from the usual densely-packed and impenetrable rows of identical conifers found in many commercial forests. Harrop Tarn (3) comes into view and its outlet is crossed over a wooden foot bridge. A little closer to the tarn is a stone ford which looks something of a challenge to cross in a vehicle. The tarn is picturesque but appears to be in the process of disappearing under encroaching weeds. It is said to be haunted by a headless spectre.

The clear path continues through the forest with the tarn on the left. After about half a kilometre the path forks to the right (4) away from a much wider, and therefore more tempting, forestry road. There is a

Plate 23: Harrop Tarn.

Plate 24: Watendlath Bridge.

signpost here pointing to the correct way. The route goes uphill and emerges into open fell side and continues in the same direction until the summit of the pass is reached (5). The path is cairned and wet underfoot although there are some strategically-placed stepping stones.

Over the top the path turns to the right and descends towards the right of Blea Tarn (6). Blea means dark which seems appropriate for this expanse of water with no trees or anything else of note. The path, intermittently wet underfoot, descends very gently towards Watendlath which is visible in the distance with its tarn. Almost level with Watendlath, and just before the ravine enclosing Raise Gill, the route turns left (7) and descends steeply on a stony, made-up path with good zigzags. At the foot of this path is the picture-postcard hamlet of Watendlath with its packhorse bridge (8) for you to admire. The route goes over the bridge and to the left and then turns right just before some woodland. It then climbs on a wide path, with the woodland to the left, towards Rosthwaite. The path reaches the top of Puddington Bank (9) and then begins the final descent to Rosthwaite. The path here is rougher and the descent longer, but the floor of the Borrowdale valley is soon reached and with it the village of Rosthwaite (10). This is on the far side of the stone bridge over the River Crook, a tributary of the Derwent. Both Rosthwaite and Watendlath have tea shops but Wythburn does not (or much of anything, really).

4: SHORT WALKS WITH BRIDGES

These are relatively easy walks which lead to bridges and may, or may not, go along part of a packhorse route. Some are there-and-back walks because it is not always possible to devise a circular walk that includes a bridge and is also short. Even though they are short they are not trivial and you will still need to have proper footwear, clothing and a map.

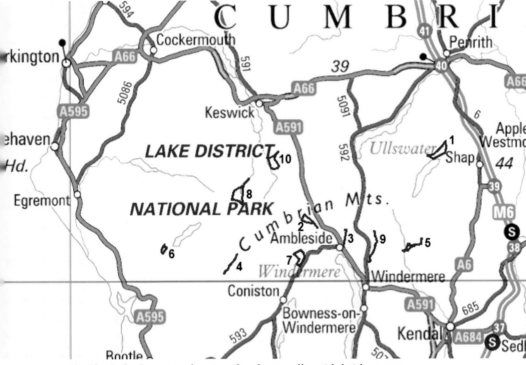

Map 40: The Lake District, showing the short walks with bridges. © *Crown Copyright and/or database right. All rights reserved. Licence number 100048757.*

1) Cawdale Bridge to Willdale
2) Far Easedale from Grasmere
3) High Sweden Bridge from
                 Ambleside
4) Lingcove Bridge from Eskdale
5) Sadgill Bridge from Kentmere

6) Scale Bridge from Nether Wasdale
7) Slater Bridge from Low Tilberthwaite
8) Stockley Bridge from Seathwaite
9) Troutbeck Park Bridge from
              Troutbeck Church
10) Watendlath Bridge from Rosthwaite

1) CAWDALE BRIDGE TO WILLDALE (and two clapper bridges)

This walk is in an empty part of the Lake District and is not the easiest to navigate so if you do get lost you are less likely to find someone able to give you directions. It is probably a good idea to take a compass. Along one stretch it has good views down Haweswater and it crosses three delightful bridges but much of the walk is over countryside with few unique identifying features which accounts for the navigational difficulties.

The walk starts from the narrow road that runs between Bampton and Moorahill Farm at the mouth of Cawdale. 'Moora' means the hill on the boggy waste. The redundant 'hill' part was added later, presumably when the original meaning had been forgotten. 'Caw' means cold, so cold valley. Willdale is probably the wild valley.

Just before Moorahill Farm the road enters an area of open fell land and it is possible to park here. Leave the road (1) and head south on a track that runs at a varying distance from the wall on the left, down to the bridge (2) over Cawdale Back. The bridge is really just an arch with no parapets and has been recently restored but is no less delightful for that. Go over the bridge and head roughly south again and shortly afterwards go over a miniature clapper bridge. Both bridges are marked on the OS map. Continue going south over marshy ground (3), with not much evidence of a path, keeping the wall on your the left and eventually go up a gentle rise to meet a clearer path (4) running at right angles. On the left, but hidden by higher ground, is a farm called Drybarrows. If necessary this is a useful navigational fix and only involves a short climb.

Turn right on the new path and follow it around the south side (5) of the hill in front. At this stage Haweswater is hidden by a series of small hills but as you progress the reservoir appears with clear views all the way to the

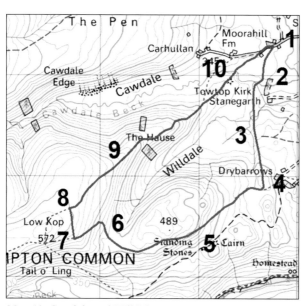

Map 41: Cawdale and Willdale. © Crown Copyright and/or database right. All rights reserved. Licence number 100048757.

Mardale end with Nan Bield Pass on the skyline. In the same direction, but much closer, is Measand Beck running down to Haweswater through a deep valley called Fordingdale Bottom. There is a wooden footbridge about 500 metres up from the lake which is another navigational aid. Further along the path it is possible to look back and see Haweswater dam at the opposite end.

The path curves to the right and crosses a flat area (6) just above the source of Willdale Beck. It then goes to the left and climbs. Pretty much at the top, but hidden from view until you are almost on it, is a disused quarry (7) with the remains of a small slate building. The path continues on, at times along a hollow, and eventually joins the return path but this junction is very indistinct and is easy to miss. In my view it is better to turn right at the quarry, which you can identify easily, and to head off due north. There is no path but fairly soon a pile of stones (8) appears on the skyline. This is on the return route. At the stones turn right and follow the sunken path in a north-easterly direction (9). At times this path is wet and overgrown and it may be better to walk alongside it. There is a quad track further on which goes in the same direction and is easier to walk on. As you descend Moorahill Farm becomes visible ahead.

Continue the descent between two conifer plantations and when the flatter ground is reached take the path that forks to the right (10). This passes by Towtop Kirk, just on the right before the river. This is an ancient circle with evidence of buildings within it. Its origins are disputed but it may have been a settlement or fort although 'Kirk' suggests a church. Beyond the circle the path goes steeply down to cross Cawdale Beck on another clapper bridge. On the far side is a track that takes you back to the road to Moorahill Farm and your car. Assuming you turn right at the quarry the walk is about six kilometres long and should take around two and a half hours.

2) FAR EASEDALE BRIDGE (Willie Goodwaller's) from Grasmere
(see also Greenup Edge and circular walk 6)
This involves just a glimpse of a bridge from the stony path leading up to Easedale Tarn and then a short cross-country walk to join what was once a packhorse route from Grasmere over Greenup Edge to the Borrowdale Valley. Easedale is derived from the Old Norse 'Asi's valley', but who Asi was is not recorded. The Wordsworths called it 'The Black Quarter' because black clouds seemed to collect there and it was in shadow late in the day.

Starting at Grasmere, where there are several car parks, leave by the Easedale Road (1) which starts just across from Sam Read's bookshop. Go gently up hill along this road past Goody Bridge; probably named after someone called Goody or Guddy. After about a kilometre, where the road turns to the right, take the path off to the left (2) through some woodland, sign-posted to Easedale Tarn. Go over a stone-covered, steel-beam bridge and then a small slate-beam bridge and follow the path that goes alongside and then through some flat fields with Easedale Beck on the right.

There is a stone, arched bridge on the right (3) leading to a farm. This is the 'New Bridge', built in 1997. The path then begins to climb with the waterfall of Sourmilk Gill ahead and to the right. Not long after the climb starts, Willie Goodwaller's bridge can be seen across some fields to the right on the land belonging to Brimmer Head Farm. This bridge is only visible for a short distance along the path at NY321086 (4), just past a large oak tree standing by itself. The bridge itself is at NY322088 (5), about 200 metres away and in the direction 25 degrees east of north. This is the only (old) bridge on this walk, and it is a distant glimpse at that, so a short pause here is well justified.

Continue climbing towards Easedale Tarn and soon the path flattens out for a short distance and then climbs again just before the tarn. The path to Far Easedale crosses the outlet of the tarn but it is worth climbing and

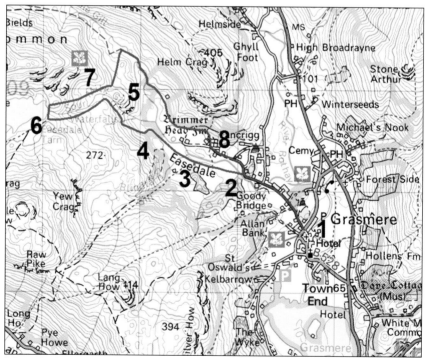

Map 42: Grasmere to Far Easedale.

Plate 25: Willie Goodwaller's Bridge, Far Easedale.

then stopping on the small hummock overlooking the tarn to admire the scenery (6). At one time there was a small stone refreshment hut here but little remains other than a large boulder that formed part of a wall.

Cross the stream on stepping stones and pick up a path that goes down on the far side of the stream. It then moves over to the left and contours round (7) over a wet area with more stepping stones to join the path that goes along the floor of the long Far Easedale Valley. Turn right onto this path and head back towards Grasmere. Go over the wooden beam bridge and follow the clear path alongside Far Easedale Gill. The path eventually becomes quite enclosed by dry stone walls and then goes between a few houses (8) to emerge into some fields. By this time it has a tarmac surface and shortly afterwards turns right when some woodland is reached. It then becomes the road that you followed up from Grasmere and tea is not far away. The walk is about seven kilometres and takes two to two and a half hours.

3) HIGH SWEDEN BRIDGE FROM AMBLESIDE
(see also Scandale Pass)
Unlike the previous walk this one has a bridge that can be examined at close quarters and crossed, several times if need be. The first part of the walk is along an old packhorse route from Ambleside to the Ullswater valley via Scandale Pass.

Starting from the centre of Ambleside walk along the main road towards Rydal and turn right up Smithy Brow (1) just before the Armitt Museum. Go up the steep road past the Golden Rule and turn left onto the Kirkstone Road. Shortly afterwards turn left again onto Sweden Bridge Lane (2). Follow this road between several houses, gradually going uphill. Go through a gate at the end of the tarmac and along a wide path between fields bounded by stone walls. Eventually the path enters woodland and passes some old quarry workings (3). On the left in a small ravine are the waterfalls of Scandale Beck. The path emerges from the woodland and High Sweden Bridge (4) is a little further on and to the left. Some time can be spent being impressed by the resilience of the arch which is clearly flattened but completely stable. It certainly has the appearance of a packhorse bridge but is not on the known route to Scandale Pass.

Plate 26: High Sweden Bridge.

When rested and refreshed cross the bridge and go uphill on the path to the left. Together with the route that you have already travelled this is part of the Fairfield Horseshoe and carries a heavy traffic of walkers in the summer. Go over a stile to reach a T-junction a little further on (5) with a path coming up from Ambleside. Turn left onto this path and go past a sheep fold on the left and then through a gap in the stone wall to descend across fell country and then fields to Low Sweden Bridge (6).

The path is increasingly clear and presents no problems as it zigzags gently downhill. Cross the bridge to reach a tarmac road that goes through

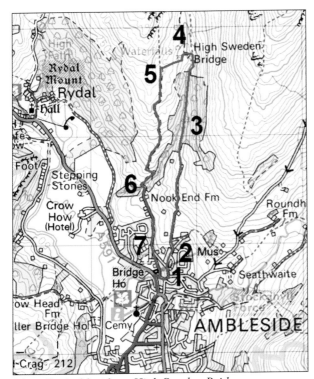

Map 43: Ambleside to High Sweden Bridge.

Nook End Farm and later on goes behind the Charlotte Mason Library (7). Charlotte Mason was an educationalist who was born in Bangor in 1842. She founded the 'House of Education' in Ambleside in 1892 to act as a training school for governesses and other teachers. It became the Charlotte Mason College after her death in 1923 and continued to train teachers. More recently it has gone through several changes of name and affiliation and became part of the University of Cumbria in 2007. The library was completed in 2003 and was built using more than 450 tonnes of Westmorland Green Elterwater slate.

The road becomes Nook Lane and takes you back to Ambleside just beside the Armitt Museum where you started. The whole walk is approximately five kilometres and takes about one and a half hours.

4) LINGCOVE BRIDGE FROM ESKDALE
(see also Esk Hause, Ore Gap and circular walks 4 and 5)
This is another valley floor path so little climbing is involved but it is hard to devise a circular route so it is a there-and-back walk. It was part of the packhorse routes from the Eskdale Valley to Borrowdale over Ore Gap and Esk Hause.

Leave your car on the large grassy verge on the Eskdale Valley road (1) just before the Hardknott Pass starts and walk a short distance towards the pass and turn left by the telephone box onto the road (2) to Brotherikeld Farm. Go to the left of the farm along a narrow path (3) close by the River

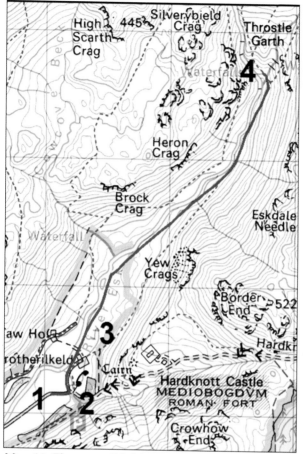

Map 44: The upper Eskdale Valley

Esk. Continue along this path keeping the river to your left as it goes through fields to reach the open fell.

Some three kilometres from where you left your car the path reaches Lingcove Bridge (4) (called Throstlegarth in Hinchliffe's book). It has all the attributes of a fine packhorse bridge and the setting is truly magnificent. It only remains to walk all the way back. There are one or two places for tea in the Eskdale Valley but a favourite one for me is Dalegarth station at the end of the Ravenglass to Eskdale Railway. You have to pay for parking but you get to watch the trains and there is always something special about a steam engine. The walk should take less than two hours.

5) SADGILL BRIDGE FROM KENTMERE
(see also Gartmore Pass, Nan Bield Pass and circular walk 8)
This walk is along an old drovers' road that took cattle and sheep between Kentmere and Longsleddale. It was part of a road system that stretched from the coast along the Eskdale Valley to Ambleside and then divided at Sadgill to go north to Shap or south to Kendal.

Starting at Kentmere (1) there is some limited parking in the village. Go over the river and along the road towards the fashionably-named Green Quarter. Before getting there turn left and head north along High Lane (2).

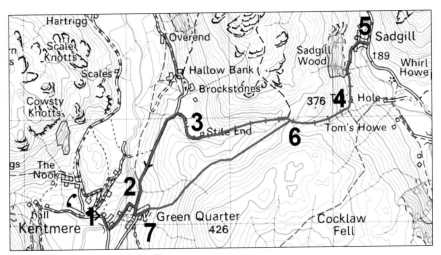

Map 45: Kentmere to Sadgill.

After about half a kilometre turn right onto an enclosed track (3) heading for Stile End. It is sign-posted to Sadgill and Long Sleddale. Currently this track is shared with motor vehicles of the cross country variety. Go gently uphill along the rough track and over the low pass at a little over 350 metres. Continue down the far side and after about half a kilometre turn left (4) through a gate and go down a stony path towards Sadgill. Towards the bottom of the valley the path enters Sadgill Woods and then passes behind a farm. Just after the farm the path turns to the right and descends to the river and Sadgill Bridge (5), a true packhorse bridge although later widened.

It is difficult to find a different way back other than turning round and heading uphill. There is, however, another route back to Kentmere from just over the top of the pass where there is a small gate to the left of the gate on the main track (6). This path, which is always easy to follow, forks to the left and gradually descends to the Green Quarter (7) in Kentmere village. The whole walk should take about two and a half hours and is about seven kilometres.

6) SCALE BRIDGE

This is quite a short walk although it can be wet and rough underfoot at times. The easiest place to park, and therefore to start, is at the small village of Nether Wasdale (1), just to the west of the foot of Wast Water. Walk down the road to Cinderdale Bridge and then turn left (2) along a track going north east towards Mill Place. It is sign-posted to Gill and Buckbarrow and goes alongside fields, through Mill Place (3) and then gently uphill. Take the right fork after Mill Place and walk with the wall to your right along a clear path for about half a kilometre. The path then forks to the right and goes through a gap in the wall by a sign post to Buckbarrow. The bridge (4) is just across the field.

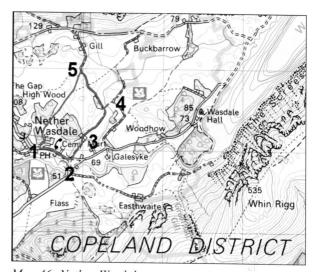

Map 46: Nether Wasdale.

After viewing the bridge either return the way you came or turn right at the signpost to Buckbarrow and follow the path in the opposite direction. At first it has trees on the left but continues on a clear path through fields in the direction of Gill. Before reaching Gill turn sharp left (5) onto the path that heads back to Nether Wasdale. This path is not always clear and is wet in places. It heads over some rough ground between Shop Wood and Churchstile Wood to descend through a camp site. Shortly afterwards it reaches the green in front of Nether Wasdale Church. The whole excursion is about three kilometres and takes an hour or so.

7) SLATER BRIDGE FROM LOW TILBERTHWAITE

Parking is difficult in Little Langdale, which is where Slater Bridge is, so perhaps a better choice is to approach it from the direction of Coniston. Leave Coniston by the A593 and after about two and a half kilometres turn left onto a minor road to Tilberthwaite. Continue on this road until you reach the double car park (1) just before and after the bridge over Yewdale Beck. Although rather isolated, this car park can get quite full. The reason for this is that there is a quarry not far up the hill above it that is much favoured for rock climbing. In fact this whole area is full of quarries, mostly no longer in production but with their effects on the landscape very evident. Just across the road from the first car park is a slate sculpture by Andy Goldsworthy built into the four walls of a sheep fold.

Abandoning your car, walk along the tarmac road past Low Tilberthwaite, admiring the galleried building on the left. Thwaite means a piece of ground cleared of trees. The Tilber part is more difficult but might mean a person's name (Tilli or Tilhere) added to *burh* which is Old English for a fortified place.

Follow the road for about half a kilometre as far as High Tilberthwaite (2). This farm was purchased by the National Trust from Beatrix Potter in 1930. In the nineteenth and early twenieth centuries Tilberthwaite was the centre of the Langdale Linen Industry set up by John Ruskin in 1883. The industry thrived until after the First World War but then collapsed in the face of cheaper foreign competition.

At the farm take the rocky path on the left (3) which goes uphill between dry stone walls. There is woodland on the right but open fell to the left with several spoil heaps. Continue on the wide and clear path over the summit and down the far side. There are some narrow paths off to the right here but they are not easy to spot and probably the best plan is to stay on the main path until it meets the valley path (4) coming down from Greenburn reservoir to the left. At this junction turn right at an acute angle and walk east along an equally wide and clear path. This descends gradually past High and then Low Hall Garth. A garth is a small, enclosed piece of land.

Shortly after Low Hall Garth there is a gate in the wall on the left which leads onto a short path to Slater Bridge (5) over the River Brathay, not far from its origin in Little Langdale Tarn. It is a double bridge with an arch of about one and a half metres leading onto a two-span clapper bridge. The bridge is narrow with a rough surface and has iron railings but is still highly photogenic and must rank as one of the prettiest of all the Lake District packhorse bridges. Crossing the bridge, probably several times, is not strictly

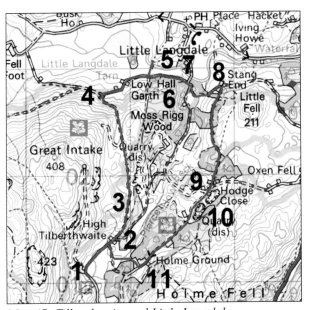

Map 47: Tilberthwaite and Little Langdale.

necessary for the walk but is virtually irresistible. Only when all the details have been taken in and fully appreciated should you return to the road and continue the walk.

Turn left on the road and continue going east for a short distance. If you wish to see a spectacular quarry take the fork to the right (6) and go through a gate and then uphill a short way to a flat area in front of a tunnel entrance. There is a stern warning here about the dangers of exploring quarries with their steep unfenced drops, deep and cold pools and chunks of rock landing on your head and you need to decide whether to proceed. Quarry aficionados, however, will be unable to resist the prospect of viewing the 'Cathedral' with its enormous and impressive enclosed space. Should you be so inclined, go through the short tunnel into the quarry with its open 'window' on the far side and large rock pillar in the centre, presumably left to hold the roof up. Back outside again you can go uphill to the west of the quarry to see the even-larger hole in the ground behind the 'Cathedral'.

Returning to the road, turn right and walk alongside the river. Very soon there is a bridge over the river and a road to the right (7). This is the road that you left at High Tilberthwaite and is the quick way back. If you wish to have a longer walk with the prospect of more quarry exploring, cross the road and wind around the edge of some woodland with the river at first close by on your left. This path joins a road going up hill to Stang End (8). Stang means a long, narrow ridge. At Stang End turn sharp right

Plate 27: Looking into Hodge Close Quarry from Parrock Quarry.

and continue on the road to the hamlet of Hodge Close (9). If you want to explore Parrock Quarry, there is a road going up hill on the left, just after you have passed the first few houses. There is then a track leading off to the right opposite a garage. With the usual warnings about the dangers of quarry exploring in mind, descend the rough track on the old incline to the quarry floor. At the far end there are two large arches leading to a deep pool in the adjacent Hodge Close Quarry. The rusted remains of a crane can be seen protruding through one of the arches. Some of the rocks in the quarry have had bolts inserted and are used for climbing.

Returning to Hodge Close continue on the road, ignoring the track leaving on the right. The road goes past the top of the enormous, water-filled pit (10) that you could see through the arches. The maximum water depth is about 32 metres and there is a tunnel entrance at 24 metres which leads to three chambers with two interconnecting tunnels. It is used by divers who explore these spaces, although this is not without risk and several have lost their lives. The main pool is the final resting place for several cars that no doubt made fine splashes as they met their ends. On the other side of the road is a parking area. Large stones now block the route to the quarry edge, no doubt to foil the car splashers. Work in the quarry stopped in the 1950s.

Continue on the road past some terraced houses and down to Holme Ground (11). Turn right here by a signpost labelled 'To High Tilberthwaite'. Go through the gate, or a narrow gap in the wall, to descend alongside some woodland and then across fields to High Tilberthwaite. It is then a short walk along the road back to Low Tilberthwaite and your car. The route is about six kilometres. The duration of the walk depends on the detours but should not be longer than about three hours.

8) STOCKLEY BRIDGE FROM SEATHWAITE

(see also Esk Hause, Sty Head Pass and circular walks 10 and 11)

If you fancy a walk along the floor of England's wettest valley, this one may be for you. It also has the advantage that parking is easy and almost unlimited along the verge of the road leading to Seathwaite Farm (1). Walk south along the road, then between farm buildings, to go straight ahead along the wide path (2) out of the farm with the River Derwent on the right. At about a kilometre from the farm the Derwent is formed by the confluence of Grains Gill and Sty Head Gill and shortly after this the path passes over Stockley Bridge (3).

This bridge was partially destroyed in the floods of 1966 and then rebuilt. The barrel survived, probably because it was several rows thick

Plates 28 and 29:   Above, Stockley Bridge following restoration and, below, in 1966 after the floods, (photograph by Owen Jones).

and therefore more resistant than the parapets. With a greater push the barrel would surely have gone too. A vertical arch resists a downward load well but has little more than the weight of its masonry to resist a sideways push. An arched dam, such as the Hoover Dam, is a bridge on its side with its arch pointing upstream and is well able to resist a downstream push, always provided that its abutments and their foundations are solid and that

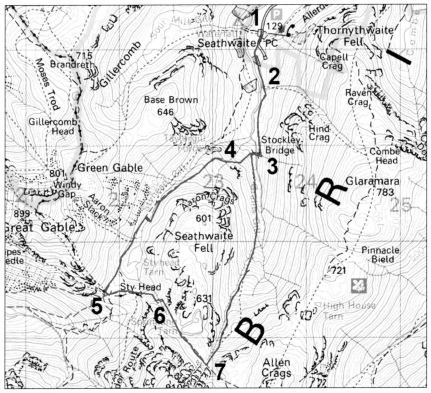

Map 48: Seathwaite to Sty Head.

the dam is securely fixed, or massive enough to stay attached, to the ground beneath it. Other types of dam just rely on their weight or pegging into underlying rock to keep them in place. Dams do well with a downwards load as well as sideways ones as they are usually of fairly solid construction. The way to destroy a dam is to produce a perforation at the base where it is under most load from the head of water and then let the water flow do the rest. Hence the need for the bouncing bombs to have a backwards spin to travel down the front of the dam and then explode at depth.*

Depending on how long a walk you want, the shortest option is to turn around after crossing the bridge and return for tea and cakes at the farmhouse in Seathwaite after about an hour or so. A longer option is to cross the bridge

---

*This is not the only reason for the backwards spin. It also made the bombs bounce better and therefore more likely to avoid any nets placed in front of the dams. Barnes Wallis, the bomb's designer, is said to have got the idea from George Edwards, later the head of the British Aircraft Corporation, who was a keen cricketer and knew the value of bowling with a back spin.

and take the path on the right (4) leading to Sty Head Pass. This is steep and rocky at first but improves after a short distance. The path eventually crosses Styhead Gill on a wooden beam bridge and continues on past Styhead Tarn to reach the pass (5). At the pass turn left onto the well-travelled path (6) between Sty Head and the Langdale Valley. Go gradually uphill past Sprinkling Tarn on the left and then turn left onto the path (7) returning to Stockley Bridge via Ruddy Gorge. This is moderately energetic for one of the short walks but gives a real flavour of the packhorse routes and should take two and a half to three hours. It is about eight kilometres long.

9) TROUTBECK PARK BRIDGE FROM TROUTBECK CHURCH

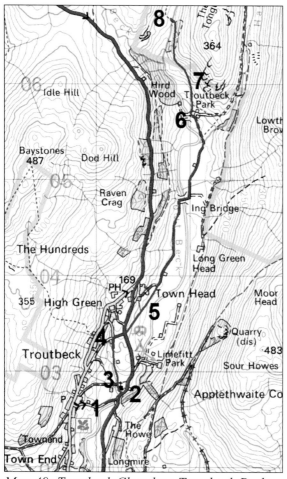

Map 49: Troutbeck Church to Troutbeck Park.

Rather like the Mosedales there are several Troutbecks in the Lake District. This one lies in the valley between Ambleside and Kentmere and carries the road (the A592) down from Kirkstone Pass to Windermere and beyond. In the upper reaches of the valley, away from the busy road, there is a large clapper bridge which is well worth a visit.

Starting at the Jesus Church (worth exploring), just off the A592 at NY413028, there is limited parking near the river (1). Go through the church yard and join the path (2) on the far side going in a north-westerly direction. About 100 metres down this path, turn right onto

Plate 30: Troutbeck Park Bridge.

another path (3) that heads almost due north between fields towards the village of Troutbeck. After about half a kilometre this joins a minor road (4). Turn right onto the road. Shortly afterwards cross the A592 and continue on a path (5) between fields and head up the valley towards Troutbeck Park (6).

The Troutbeck valley was heavily forested in early medieval times and was used for hunting deer. In time the hunting became confined to roughly the area now farmed by Troutbeck Park. This farm was once owned by Beatrix Potter and was left by her to the National Trust, whose plaque you can see on the wall. Go through the farm and follow the rather wet path (7) that goes to the west of The Tongue. After about a kilometre it crosses Trout Beck over a large clapper bridge (8) which has no less than five waterways. It is unclear when and why such a large bridge was built here as the path is a minor one and is not on a known packhorse route. Perhaps it is just for farm use. Nevertheless it is here and deserves to be admired. The path beyond goes along the length of the valley and there is no short route back so perhaps the best thing is just to retrace your steps, a distance of almost ten kilometres in all. It takes two to three hours there and back.

10) WATENDLATH BRIDGE FROM ROSTHWAITE
(see also Watendlath and circular walk 12)

Rosthwaite, "the clearing where horses are kept", was the main packhorse centre in the southern end of the Borrowdale Valley. These days it is a pleasant little village that has a dog's leg on the narrow road going through it which acts as an effective speed control. The route over to Watendlath was used by packhorse trains coming and going to Wythburn at the southern end of Thirlmere. What is now a tarmac road from Watendlath towards Keswick was probably also a packhorse route as was the road along the floor of the Borrowdale Valley.

Coming into Rosthwaite from Keswick there is a car park on the road going off to the right just before the bend and another through the village, just beyond the Scafell Hotel. From either car park, walk back into the village (1) and then onto the road towards Keswick. Almost immediately turn right at a sign post to Stonethwaite and Watendlath and go between two small fields to cross the bridge over Stonethwaite Beck. Turn left and head uphill (2), shortly afterwards going along a curious raised footpath over two small streams. The path then heads up the side of the Borrowdale Valley. It is rocky in places but is always obvious and easy to negotiate. Towards the top, where the path is joined by another from the left, is the Resting Stone (3), a convenient spot to, well, rest.

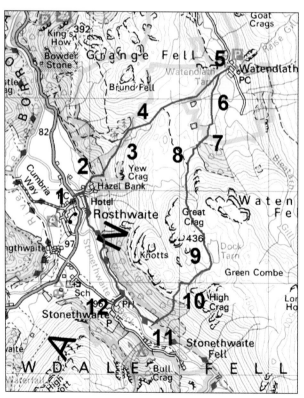

Map 50: Rosthwaite to Watendlath and Stonethwaite.

The path reaches a maximum height of about 320 metres

at Puddingstone Bank (4). Readyhough says that boulders of a rounded shape are often referred to as pudding stones because their shape suggests a pudding but I was unable to see an obvious candidate. Over the top, the surface of the path improves and there is a pleasant and gentle descent into the hamlet of Watendlath (5). The path leads straight to the delectable packhorse bridge over the outlet of Watendlath Tarn. Watendlath is a popular spot for visitors because of its setting and its typical Lake District farm buildings, now largely owned by the National Trust. There is a car park so the walk can be started here if preferred. Perhaps of more interest on a hot day, there is also a tea shop.

After admiring the bridge the shortest way back is the way you came. The total distance is about five kilometres. An alternative, but more challenging, way back is to go south on the path (6) alongside Watendlath Tarn, sign-posted to Dock Tarn. This is a clear path which gently rises between stone walls with some pollarded trees on the left. A little way beyond the end of Watendlath Tarn the path turns to the right (7) and heads uphill. There are several small metal sign posts indicating the route. Just beyond the trees the path divides into two. Take the left branch (8), sign-posted to Dock Tarn and go along the narrow, made-up path through some wet land.

The path then climbs quite steeply with Great Crag on the right. At the top of the short climb the path goes to the left and starts a rocky descent to Dock Tarn (9), "the mountain pool where water plants grow," most likely water lilies, which are still there. Leaving the tarn the path gently descends towards Stonethwaite. The descent becomes more steep with the long waterfall of Willigrass Gill (Willy's land beside the stream) on the left (10). The made-up path then enters woodland and becomes a steep zigzag until it reaches the floor of the valley where it joins the Cumbria Way from Langstrath. Turn right here (11) and head towards Stonethwaite. There is a pub and a tea shop over the bridge (12) in Stonethwaite, should you need them, otherwise continue on the clear path for another kilometre or so until you reach Rosthwaite. The longer walk is about eight kilometres and takes about three hours.

5: LONG CIRCULAR WALKS

What follows is a description of twelve circular walks, mainly along pack-horse routes, each of which is suitable for a day's outing as it gets back to where it started from. As with the there-and-back pass walks they are generally quite long. It is in the nature of these routes that they go from a valley to a ridge, along the ridge then back down another valley usually with a connecting bit at the end to take you back to the starting point. That means walking some distance, both along the packhorse routes and along the connecting paths, which may, or may not be, old packhorse routes, and doing at least one climb. Nevertheless they make excellent walks and offer the chance of views when the tops are covered in mist. I have tried, not always successfully, to include a bridge or two. Often the bridge can be seen without doing much of the walk, but think how much more satisfied you will feel if you have done the whole thing.

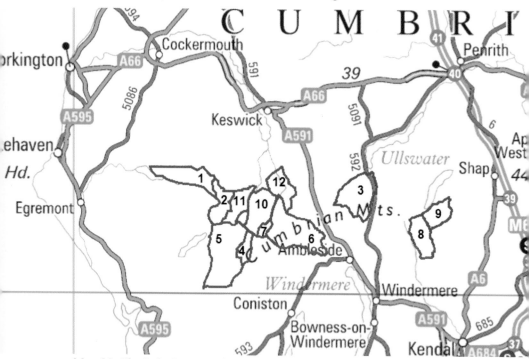

Map 51: The Lake District, showing the long circular walks.

1) Buttermere to Ennerdale

2) Buttermere to Wasdale Head

3) Dovedale to Patterdale

4) Eskdale to Ore Gap and
   Esk Hause

5) Eskdale to Wasdale Head and
   Burn Moor

6) Grasmere to Langstrath and
   Langdale

7) Langdale to Langstrath

8) Mardale Head to Kentmere and
   Sadgill

9) Mardale Head to Swindale

10) Seathwaite to Langstrath

11) Seathwaite to Wasdale Head

12) Stonethwaite to Greenup Edge
   and Watendlath

1) BUTTERMERE TO ENNERDALE (no bridges)
(see also Floutern Pass, Mosedale and Scarth Gap)

Buttermere, "the lake by the good grazing" had lots of packhorse connections. Lorton and Rosthwaite are all joined by roads now but the routes over from Ennerdale Bridge via Floutern Pass and to Wasdale Head via Scarth Gap and Black Sail are still pleasures to walk. This circle connects Scarth Gap with Floutern but to do this involves a long (three hour) trek through the Ennerdale forest.

There are several car parks in Buttermere village and several places for refreshments. Take the path that goes through Wilkinsyke (William's syke or stream) Farm (1) down to the lake side. The packhorse route probably more or less followed what is now the road to Honister but the lakeside is

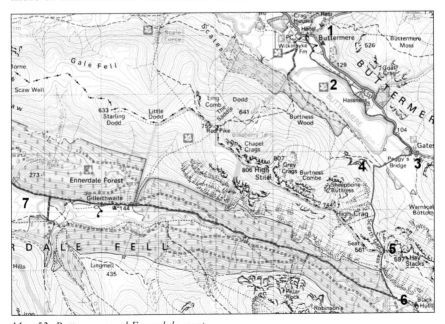

Map 52: Buttermere and Ennerdale, east.

vastly more pleasant. It even has a short tunnel (2). This is the 35 metre-long Hassness Tunnel, a remarkably self-indulgent piece of civil engineering. It was constructed in the nineteenth century by George Benson, the land owner, to save himself the trouble of having to climb over a rocky promontory on his lake side stroll. On the other hand it provided employment and saves us the trouble as well.

Towards the end of the lake, the path evaporates and the road has to be followed to Gatesgarth Farm (3). Go through the farm on the sign-posted path to the far side of the lake. Shortly after crossing Warnscale Beck on Peggy's Bridge either go straight up Buttermere Fell or, like the horses probably did, take a zigzag to the right (4). Continue up the obvious and increasingly stony path to Scarth Gap (5). At the top pause to admire the view of some of the most impressive of the Lake District mountains on the far side of the Ennerdale Valley: Great Gable, Kirk Fell and Pillar. Even the modest mountain on the left, Haystacks, has achieved fame as Wainwright's favourite. On the right is Seat leading to a ridge walk that takes in High Crag, High Stile and Red Pike and ultimately leads to Floutern Pass. This is a shorter but perfectly respectable alternative route which involves more climbing and has fine views but does miss out the western end of Floutern Pass and the descent into Ennerdale.

At the top of Scarth Gap go straight ahead on an indistinct path and then start to go down into the Ennerdale Valley. Ennerdale has been a victim of the forestry industry and you are about to see a lot of that over the next three hours or so. Descend to the valley floor alongside the dismal tree stumps and turn right (6) when the path to the Black Sail Hut is reached. You then have a long trek, not on a packhorse route, through Ennerdale Forest with the River Liza on your left. Eventually the view opens up a little with a marshy area on the left (7) and then opens up much more with the start of Ennerdale Water.

The path continues on by the lake side until pretty much the end of the lake is reached. You then need to find your way to Whins. On the OS map there is a straight path going up from the lake shore but it is difficult to find (see Floutern Pass). It is easier to use a more devious route off to the right at the point where the lakeside path takes a ninety degree turn to the left (8). This subsequently goes past Beckfoot and then joins the road (9) up to Whins.

A little before Whins, turn right (10) to go up the hillside on a muddy track between fields, gradually rising until the open fell is reached. Continue along a fairly clear path, which was a packhorse route, with Gill Beck on the right until the summit of the pass (11) is reached at a little over 400 metres. Floutern Tarn appears on the right. Continue descending, with

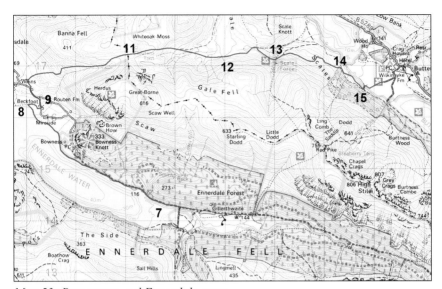

Map 53: Buttermere and Ennerdale, west.
© *Crown Copyright and/or database right. All rights reserved. Licence number 100048757.*

Hen Comb on the left, into the increasingly boggy Mosedale. Around here a packhorse route from Loweswater joins from the left. Perhaps it had been unusually wet when I did the walk but this area was so marshy as to be almost impassible.

A better choice is to go more to the right (12) and up and along the flank of Gale Fell although even this is wet. Continue on down in the direction of Crummock Water joining, and at some point crossing, Scale Beck (13). There are one or two rather wet paths along the side of Crummock Water going in the direction of Buttermere which seem to consolidate into one further on (14). When this path reaches the fields between Buttermere and Crummock Water turn left (15), go over Scale Bridge and along the path between the fields separating the two lakes to reach Buttermere village. The whole route covers about 26 kilometres and takes seven or eight hours.

2) BUTTERMERE TO WASDALE HEAD (Wasdale Head Bridge)
(see also, Black Sail Pass, Burn Moor, Moses Trod, Scarth Gap and circular walks 1, 5 and 11)
This is a fairly long walk with considerable height gain but is generally on good and clear paths. It can be shortened by turning left just before the top of the Black Sail Pass and skirting around Kirk Fell to meet Moses Trod between Kirk Fell and Great Gable. If you do this you will miss the

delightful and elegant packhorse bridge at Wasdale Head, but you may
have seen it before. Even so you will still get a taste for the passes in this
part of the Lake District.

Start from the car park (1) just off the road at the eastern end of
Buttermere at Gatesgarth farm. Cross the road towards the lake and take
the path labelled 'To the Lakeside' next to the farm yard. This path (2)
goes across the end of the lake to the far side of the valley. Go through a
gate and then up a steep path labelled 'Ennerdale via Scarth Gap'.

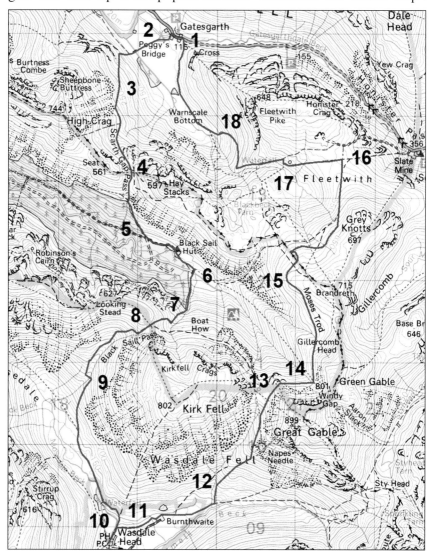

Map 54: Buttermere and Wasdale Head.

Alternatively fork to the right and do a small zigzag and conserve your strength. Both paths join a little way up the hillside. Continue up the steep and stony path (3) and over a small wooden bridge, through another gate and follow the path as it ascends, then flattens and ascends again towards the top of the pass.

The top of Scarth Gap (4) is eventually reached with Hay Stacks to the left, Seat to the right and Kirk Fell in front of you across the far side of the Ennerdale Valley. Go straight ahead. The path is indistinct here but becomes clearer as you begin to descend.

Great Gable becomes visible at the head of the valley on the left and Pillar Rock is a little to the right on the far side of the valley. At the time of writing this area is marred by the tree felling which has taken place immediately to the right of the path which has left an area which looks as if it has been ravaged by a small nuclear event. No doubt much of the rest of Ennerdale awaits a similar fate. At the bottom of the valley turn left (5) onto a wide path leading to the Black Sail Youth Hostel, the closest thing we have to an Alpine hut. All the inmates have cycled or walked to get here which produces a camaraderie which has disappeared from hostels where the clientele arrive painlessly in their cars.

After leaving the hut continue along the path which heads towards the top of the valley while at the same time descending towards the river. Cross the wooden bridge (6) over the river. My accompanying dog pre-ferred to swim across but even on a hot day the water of these rivers is sur-prisingly cold. Begin to ascend the far side of the valley towards the Black Sail Pass. There is a short scramble (7) which made me wonder how heav-ily-laden packhorses would have managed. Perhaps there is a detour but I did not see it. After the scramble the path moves over to the right. At the top of the pass (8) there is an iron gate. Carry straight on and descend towards Mosedale. This is the valley that leads into Wasdale. The path crosses a stream (9) and continues to descend with the river on your right. Wast Water comes into view towards the right. Continue on the path and fork right (10) towards Wasdale Head to arrive at the famous packhorse bridge. Sadly there is no genuine reason to go over it to continue the walk but do you really need one? A delightful and elegant bridge in a beautiful setting and well worth the walk to see it.

Returning after lunch, retrace your steps to the start of the Black Sail path and then take the right fork labelled 'Great Gable and Sty Head'. This path (11) goes over a series of small wooden bridges and then to the left of some farm buildings. Cross a bigger wooden bridge which goes over what looks as though it could be a formidable river after heavy rain fall. When I crossed the weather had been dry for some time and there was just a small stream with only the wide and eroded banks to indicate what it might have been in different circumstances. Turn left almost immediately after the bridge and head up the path (12) towards the gap between Gable and Kirk Fell. This is the path known as Moses Trod. At this point it is quite steep and tiring to climb but there is no alternative. Go through a gate in a wall and continue up the hill with a ravine on the left. Later the path veers to the left and, thankfully, becomes less steep as it goes across the scree.

At the top of the pass (13) the path goes to the right and uphill towards the summit of Gable but not for long as it then passes over the edge of the Ennerdale Valley and begins to descend. This is the highest point of the walk. The Black Sail Hut is just visible to the left in the valley floor and the path over Scarth Gap can be seen, much lower than where you are now. Follow the path down to Stone Cove and around the top of Ennerdale. Cross the stream (14) at the apex of the valley and begin the gentle climb up to the far side. Leave the rim of the valley and follow the path as it moves to the right (15) and then over a stile to join another path from the right coming down from Green Gable and Brandreth. Go left and descend towards the remains of the drum house (16) on the old quarry railway.

At the drum house turn left and follow the track of the old tramway downhill towards the old, and now some new, quarry workings. Go past a collection of old slate-built quarry buildings on the right (17) and descend towards Buttermere, keeping the river on your left. Soon a path joins from the left. There is an old slate mine on the left on the far side of the river. Continue the descent (18) on the clear but stony path. Buttermere becomes visible on the right and eventually the path flattens out on the valley floor and the car park is soon reached. The route is about nineteen kilometres long and takes seven hours or so to walk.

3) DOVEDALE TO FAIRFIELD AND PATTERDALE (Hartsop Bridge, with a small detour)
(see also Scandale and Grisedale Passes)
This walk links two passes, Scandale and Grisedale, that led north east from the central Lake District to the Ullswater Valley. The link between the tops of the two passes goes over one of the Lake District's highest mountains so you need reasonable weather and some stamina to attempt it. The link in the Ullswater Valley can be by road but there is a more pleasant, although slightly longer, alternative.

The walk starts at the car parks (1) on either side of Goldrill Beck, the outlet to Brothers Water. The gold refers to marsh marigolds. Take the clear path (2) that heads south along the west side of Brothers Water, the smallest of the lakes. Continue on the path to Hartsop Hall (3). This started as a

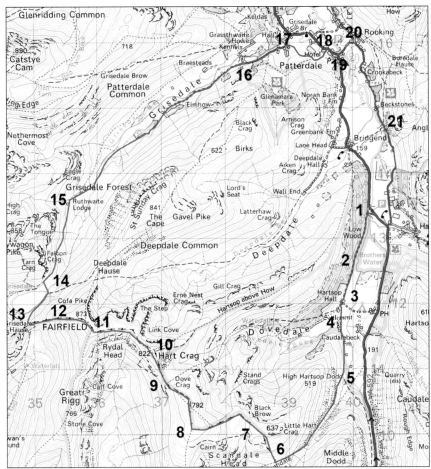

Map 55: Dovedale to Patterdale.

fifteenth century manor house but is now a farm owned, since 1947, by the National Trust having been acquired by the Treasury in lieu of death duties. It shows an interesting mix of building styles illustrating its enlargement over the years. On the hillside above the hall are some disused mines, last worked in 1942.

Shortly after the hall, fork left through a gate next to some farm buildings. There is a sign post here to Scandale. When I did this walk there was a large bull blocking the way. Although he was with several of his girl friends and was therefore probably fairly content with the world I felt it wiser to make a small detour. Go across the field (4) and over the wide wooden bridge. Continue on with the stone wall on the left with good views of Kirkstone Pass ahead. The path contours around the side of High

Hartsop Dodd and then starts to climb towards the open fell. Wainwright says that the summit of High Hartsop Dodd is uninteresting and has little distinction but it looks pretty impressive from here. The path goes through two gates with a sheep enclosure between them (5) and then climbs steadily to the top of the pass (6) with Caiston Beck on the left. Scandale means a short valley, which it certainly is compared with Grisedale, and the top is soon reached.

Turn right on the top of the pass just before the wall and follow it along in a north-westerly direction (7). Soon the wall disappears to be replaced with fence posts. Continue to follow these posts as the path turns to the left and climbs, eventually to join the highway along the Fairfield Horseshoe (8). This is much more heavily walked than the route so far travelled. Continue on this clear path which has a couple of climbs and descents before it finally reaches the summit of Fairfield. The first climb is to Dove Crag (9) which seems insignificant from this side but in fact has an impressive escarpment facing Dovedale, the side valley where this route started. Below Dove Crag, just off the route up from Dovedale, is the Priest's Hole. This is a cave some three metres deep once used as a hiding place for priests. The second summit is Hart Crag (10) which is much more rocky but presents no problems to the walker. There are good views to the left down the almost-perfect U-shaped valley of Rydal Fell with Windermere and the sea in the distance. It is followed by a short, but quite steep, descent to Link Hause and then the final climb to Fairfield.

The summit of Fairfield (11) is large and rounded with two stone shelters and it is easy to become disorientated on it in poor weather. I once demonstrated this with two friends and instead of continuing along the Horseshoe route to Rydal took the path to Grisedale Hause and then down past the Great Tongue to Grasmere and had a long walk home. As well as the way up from Scandale, there are three other paths off the summit, one to Great Rigg and onto the Horseshoe, another to St Sunday Crag and then Patterdale and the third to Grisedale Hause, which is the one we want. The latter starts from near the shelters, is cairned and heads almost due west. It is steep and eroded in places (12) and needs some care. More and more of Grisedale Tarn appears below and to the right during the descent and the Hause is reached quite quickly.

Turn right at the Hause (13) and follow the path that goes to the east of Grisedale Tarn. This is part of the packhorse route from Grasmere to Patterdale that goes down the long Grisedale Valley. At the far end of the tarn cross Grisedale Beck using the stepping stones, join the path coming down from Dollywaggon Pike near to the Brothers' Parting Stone (see Grisedale Hause, page 71) (14) and descend into the valley. The path is obvious all the way down but divides below Ruthwaite Lodge (15) to go on either side of the beck. Both paths eventually join at the point where the tarmac road starts but I have only used the one on the right. From the Hause it takes about two hours to reach the mouth of the valley.

At the end of the path (16), join the the tarmac road heading towards Patterdale and the Ullswater valley. Patterdale means Patrick's valley and its church is appropriately dedicated to Saint Patrick. Ullswater, or Ulf's lake, is the second longest of the lakes and is home to the char and schelly among other fish. It has four islands but in spite of this was used by Donald Campbell to establish the world water speed record of 202 miles per hour (326 kilometres per hour) on 23 July 1955. Some of its water is removed via a tunnel 2.74 kilometres long to Heltondale and eventually to Manchester.

The quickest way back is to continue to the end of this minor road and then turn right onto the main road (A592) and head towards Kirkstone Pass and the car park at Brothers Water. It is a tedious walk as the footpath moves from one side of the road to the other many times. Much nicer, and safer, is to walk along a path through fields and then on a minor road on the far side of Goldrill Beck. The first detour starts on the right, just before the Patterdale sports ground, about 200 metres up from the junction with the main road, where the Grisedale road turns to the left (17). It has a public footpath sign and a series of posts marking the way as it forks left through a small gate and then across a field. It later forks to the right in some woodland and emerges onto the main road (18) almost opposite the While Lion pub. Turn right onto the road and walk about 50 metres and then turn left (19) and cross the bridge over Goldrill Beck and head for the hamlet of Rooking (20). The name is derived from the Old English 'ruh', or rough, and 'kinn', a slope, presumably the hillside above it, and nothing to do with rooks as I had thought. Wordsworth bought an estate here in 1806, intending to build a house but never did and sold the land in 1834. Turn right in Rooking and walk along the quiet road in the direction of Hartsop. A few hundred metres after passing through Beckstones the road turns to the right to cross Deepdale Bridge, another possible way back.

Nicer though, is to fork left (21) and head gently uphill, perhaps not a welcome thought at this stage in the walk but the height gain is relatively little, and continue along the path. It is shortly joined by one coming down from Boredale Hause and ends on the narrow road to Hartsop (22). There is a packhorse bridge well worth seeing on the far side of this delightful village. Turning to the right, away from the village, is the main road and turning right here gets you back to your car. The walk is about 21 kilometres long and takes seven or eight hours.

4) ESKDALE TO ORE GAP AND ESK HAUSE (Lingcove Bridge)

(see also Esk Hause, Ore Gap, Rossett Gill Pass and circular walk 5)

This walk goes along two of the most remote and spectacular valleys in the Lake District, one of which can be quite wet. It is linked by a short stretch of the Wasdale to Langdale route and provides a fine day's outing.

Start at the informal car park (1) at the foot of the western end of Hardknott Pass and walk towards the pass for a short distance before

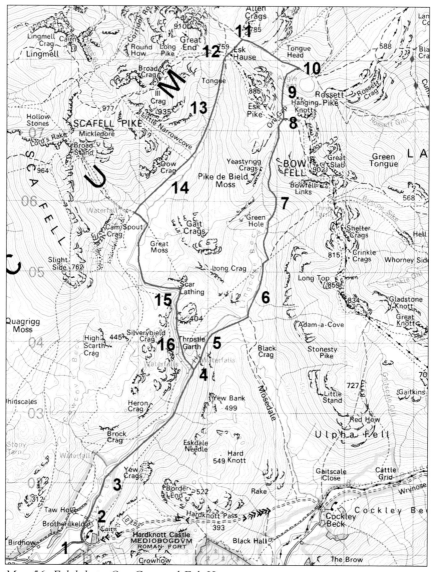

Map 56: Eskdale to Ore Gap and Esk Hause.

turning left at a telephone kiosk to go through a gate and onto a farm road. This leads to Brotherikeld Farm (2). Go to the left of the farm and along the path (3) that clings to the side of the River Esk. It is an easy path to follow and goes for about three kilometres along the gently rising valley floor, never straying very far from the river. At the point where the Esk is joined by Lingcove Beck stop to admire Lingcove Bridge (4). It is not necessary to cross it at this stage but the temptation to do so will probably be too great to resist. You will return over the bridge some hours later but perhaps by then your appreciative faculties will have been dulled by tiredness so make the most of it now.

Go along the path (5) to the right of the bridge, with Lingcove Beck on your left, and climb the hill in front. In places the path is rocky and then boggy but there are no great problems. At the top of the rise the path flattens out (6) and enters a valley which runs almost exactly north with Crinkle Crags on the right and Lingcove Beck still on the left. Continue along the valley floor. At times the path is unclear and some streams have to be crossed. To the right there is a gap between Crinkle Crags and Bowfell but continue straight on towards Ore Gap which is straight ahead and then start to climb (7) with Yeastyrigg Gill to the left.

After a stiff climb the top of the pass (8) is reached between Bowfell and Esk Pike, the highest point of this walk at about 770 metres. Continue down the far side of the pass (9) with Angle Tarn to the right until you reach the thoroughfare that runs between Sty Head and the Langdale Valley. Turn left (10) and climb to the col (11) between Esk Hause and Allen Crags. When this is reached turn left and head up the hill a short distance to Esk Hause at 759 metres (12) and start the descent (13) to the Great Moss. This is a magnificent route although narrow in places at first. It opens out to reveal one of the great valleys of the Lake District with the massive bulk of Ill Crag and Scafell Pike to the right.

On the valley floor the route (14) goes to the right of the stream that will become the River Esk and crosses Little Narrowcove Beck to stay close to the base of the Pike. The valley itself is very wet and can be a challenge to cross. At some stage though it does have to be crossed and the other side of the valley reached. The actual path seems to vary according to local conditions but I have generally taken one that goes to the west of Scar Lathing and close to the left bank of the river. Having reached the other side of the valley follow the meander of the river round (15) and then start the descent to Lingcove Bridge with the river in a ravine on the right. The path (16) descends quite steeply to the bridge and you know your way back from there. It is about eighteen kilometres long and takes between five and six hours.

5) ESKDALE TO WASDALE HEAD AND BURN MOOR (Lingcove, Wasdale Head, Boot and Doctor Bridges)

(see also Burn Moor, Esk Hause, Ore Gap, Sty Head Pass, short walk 4 and circular walk 4)

Boot has a delightful bridge and, almost as good, it has an old water mill right next to it. Parking here is very limited and it might be better to start at the roadside car park (1) at the foot of Hardknott Pass. From here take the farm road by the telephone box just across the main road and a little towards Hardknott Pass and head for Brotherikeld Farm. Go to the left of the farm (2) and walk along the path (3) that keeps close to the left bank of the River Esk. This is a clear path which slowly rises towards the end of the valley where Lingcove Beck meets the Esk.

Go over the delightful Lingcove Bridge (4) and up the steep climb with the Esk in a ravine on the left. At the top follow the bend of the river round to the right and then the left to emerge into the Great Moss (5). Make your way across this wide and very wet valley and at some point cross the Esk to reach the Scafell Pike side. Continue on the flat valley floor with the base of Scafell Pike on your left. Cross the stream marked Little Narrowcove on the OS map (6) and climb up the narrow valley towards Esk Hause. This widens out towards the top and rewards the walker with views in all directions. Go over Esk Hause (7) and then down to the well-worn path between the Langdales and Sty Head. Turn left onto this path (8) towards Sty Head, soon passing Sprinkling Tarn on the right.

At Sty Head turn left onto the old packhorse route (9) to the south of the modern path to Wasdale Head. It starts about 50 metres beyond the stretcher box in the direction of Wasdale Head, and has a small cairn to mark the v-shaped hollow that the path follows. Further down the path becomes clearer and crosses Spouthead Gill just before it joins Piers Gill to form Lingmell Beck. Ultimately the route joins Moses Trod (10), over from Honister. Continue down the valley to admire the packhorse bridge at Wasdale Head (11) and to recover.

When recovered head south out of Wasdale Head on the road and where it turns to the right, just past the parking area, go straight ahead (12) across the fields on the valley floor. It is sign-posted to Eskdale but warns that the area is liable to flooding. Shortly afterwards it is easy to see why as a (usually) dry river bed has to be crossed. An alternative is to go a little further on the road and turn left just after the camp site. On the original route, turn left after the camp site and go through the middle of three gates and on through some woodland which encloses a climbing hut called Brackenclose. Start to climb up the hillside past Fence Wood (13) on the right. Shortly after passing the wood the path turns to the left (14) and climbs less steeply. It is easy

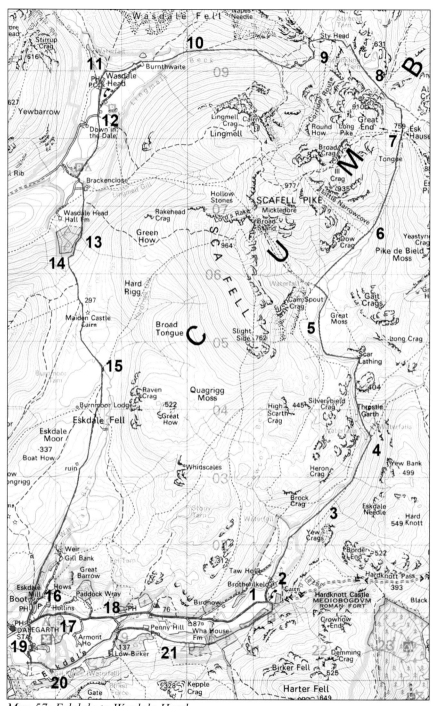

Map 57: Eskdale to Wasdale Head.

to miss this turn off as another path, which ultimately goes up Illgill Head, continues straight ahead and seems to be the correct path. This is a problem on Burn Moor as there are several paths and few navigational points and it is easy to head in the wrong direction. Eventually, at the top of the pass, Burnmoor Tarn becomes visible with Burnmoor Lodge at its far end. This is useful confirmation that you are on the correct path.

Continue down and then cross a wide, wet area at the head of the tarn. Go over Bulatt Bridge (15) and continue going roughly south ignoring paths off to Burnmoor Lodge and Eskdale Moor on the right and down to Whillan Beck on the left. The latter leads to a bridge over the beck which is another useful marker. The correct path is wet and stony in places and gradually goes down to the fields of the Eskdale Valley. It becomes more enclosed by a dry stone wall and some woodland on the left with Whillan Beck some distance below. Almost at Boot the path is joined on the right (16) by another from Miterdale.

The path enters Boot next to the old water mill and then goes over the packhorse bridge and through the village to join the main valley road. Turn left here and walk back along the road (17) to where you left your car. It will take almost an hour. About one kilometre along this road there is a small road off to the right down which the Doctor Bridge (18) goes over the Esk. I expect by now you have lost interest in detours and bridges but it's there for another time. One of the pubs on the way is called the Woolpack Inn and has a painting of a packhorse as its sign. The whole walk takes nine to ten hours and is about 28 kilometres.

For those not totally exhausted by the time they reach Boot, and assuming there is still some daylight, a pleasant alternative to the valley road is to walk along a path by the River Esk. It adds a kilometre, and about half an hour, but you cross the Doctor Bridge without having to make a detour. Instead of turning left where the side road from Boot meets the main valley road, go straight ahead along a wide track (19) signposted to St. Catherine's, Eskdale Parish Church. The church is on the right just before the river. There has been a church here for a long time, perhaps since the fifteenth century, but the one you see was largely built in 1881. It was the end of the coffin road from Wasdale Head.

Just past the church, turn left and walk along the river bank taking the upper of two paths, the lower one leading to a wooden foot bridge. The path (20) is easy to follow and eventually leads to the Doctor Bridge (18). Go over the bridge, possibly examining its underside to see the older arch, and go straight ahead towards Penny Hill Farm. This was the residence of the original 'Doctor'. Go through the farm yard, or avoid it on a signed detour, and continue walking roughly east (21) on a less-clear path through

Plate 31: Doctor Bridge, showing the join underneath - the old part is on the left.

fields and deciduous woodland. After about two and a half kilometres the path goes to the left to cross Hardknott Gill, a tributary of the Esk, on the tiny Jubilee Bridge. At the top of the bank turn left on the road coming down from the passes and your car should be about 200 metres away.

6) GRASMERE TO LANGSTRATH AND LANGDALE (Far Easedale or Willie Goodwaller's bridge)
(see also Greenup Edge, Stake Pass, short walk 2 and circular walk 12)
Leave Grasmere on the road to Easedale Tarn (1) just across from Sam Read's bookshop. Go uphill on this road for about a kilometre, past Goody Bridge, and then as the road turns to the right in some woodland (2) you have a choice. If you turn left, over two beam bridges, towards Easedale Tarn you will be able to see, from a distance, the only packhorse bridge on this route. As there is only a glimpse of a bridge, and this walk is long enough already, you might be inclined to avoid this detour. For the stout hearted though, follow the rough, stony, and at times wet, path through the fields (3) with Easedale Beck on the right and then uphill with the water-fall of Sourmilk Gill clearly visible ahead and to the right. From this path (4) it is possible to see Willie Goodwaller's Bridge on the right (5) on pri-vate land belonging to Brimmer Head Farm. It is only visible for a short distance on the path (see Short Walk 2, page 114) and you need to know

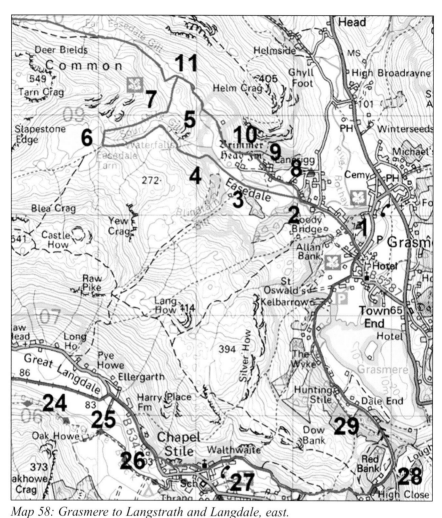

Map 58: Grasmere to Langstrath and Langdale, east.

where to look. Continue up to Easedale Tarn and then turn right at the
Tarn's outlet (6) and cross the river to descend around the side of Cockly
Crag and Stenner's Crag (7) to the path along Far Easedale.

The original packhorse route went from Grasmere straight to Far
Easedale, and you can certainly go that way. Instead of turning left onto
the path to Easedale Tarn (2), continue along the road towards Far
Easedale, passing between fields (8) and then some houses. Go up the
enclosed stony lane (9) towards Helm Cragg and then turn left after the
iron gate to go along the wet and stony path that leads into the Far
Easedale valley (10).

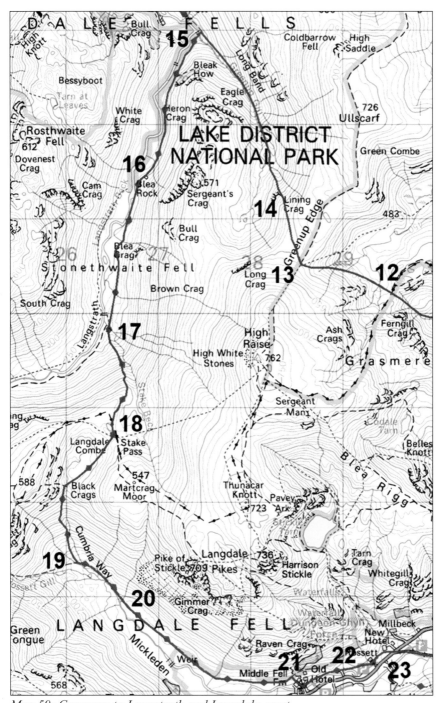

Map 59: Grasmere to Langstrath and Langdale, west.
© *Crown Copyright and/or database right. All rights reserved. Licence number 100048757.*

About a kilometre further on, the route crosses a wooden beam bridge and shortly afterwards is joined by the path from Easedale Tarn (11). Continue to walk roughly west along the clear path, eventually to climb up the head of the valley and into a wet bowl at the top (12). This is easily passable after dry weather but, if not, a small detour to the left may help. At the far side of the bowl climb up to Greenup Edge (13). Go over the top detouring around the many wet patches and down the far side towards Stonethwaite. This is a clear path with excellent views, particularly from the rocky outcrop called Lining Crag (14).

At the bottom of the pass where Greenup Gill meets Langstrath Beck turn left to go over a wooden footbridge (15) and walk along the floor of the Langstrath valley in pretty much a southerly direction (16). It is a good path, although undulating at times, eventually crossing the wooden bridge over Stake Beck (17) after about three kilometres. Turn left here and head up the zigzags to Stake Pass. Both Langstrath and Stake Pass were pack-horse routes. It takes some time to cross the wide summit of Stake Pass (18) to begin the descent on the made-up zigzag path to the head of the Langdale Valley (19), another packhorse route. Turn left when the valley floor is reached and walk along the wide path (20) south east and then east with Mickleden Beck on your right. Continue on until the back of the Old Dungeon Ghyll Hotel (21) is reached. You can either go down to the road and walk along it as far as the New Dungeon Ghyll Hotel, walk through the fields on the valley floor on a path (22) starting from the far side of the car park (see Rossett Gill Pass, page 89), which might be the nicest option, or walk along a rather up-and-down path on the valley side. The latter is reached by going a short way up hill just before the Old Hotel is reached.

Just before the New Hotel is the Stickle Barn which can provide a welcome mug of tea. At the New Hotel (23) go down to the car park on the far side of the road and leave it at the far left corner and walk along the wide path (24). This is a more pleasant alternative than the main valley road. This respite does not last long, however, and the path joins the road at a farm called Robinson Place. Turn right (25) and go along the road but branch off left just before Chapel Stile to go up a rather enclosed path (26) which leads into a disused quarry.

After the quarry the path joins the road (27) from Chapel Stile to Grasmere via High Close (28). After High Close keep to the left and walk downhill with Grasmere (the lake, that is) on the right through some trees. Continue on this road (29) until Grasmere Village is reached. There are lots of places for tea and cakes in Grasmere but by the time you get there they will probably all be closed, at least they always have been by the time that I have staggered in. This is a long walk but a very varied one that you can feel happy and satisfied to have completed. Depending on your choices the walk is about 30 kilometres long and takes around nine hours.

7) LANGDALE TO LANGSTRATH (no bridges)
(see also Ore Gap, Rossett Gill Pass, Stake Pass, and circular walk 6)
This is part of the important route from the west coast to the central Lake District at Ambleside. From the walkers' point of view the most interesting part is from the Langdale Valley to Wasdale Head but this is a long trek if you have to do both directions on the same day. A more realistic walk is to turn right after Rossett Gill Pass and go down to Langstrath and then back to the Langdale Valley over Stake Pass but even this involves two climbs.

The nearest starting point is the public car park at the Old Dungeon Gill Hotel but this fills up quickly in the summer. In this case an alternative is the larger car park next to the Stickle Barn which is in turn next to the New Dungeon Gill Hotel. This adds about fifteen minutes walk in each direction. From the car park at the Stickle Barn (1) there are two paths to the

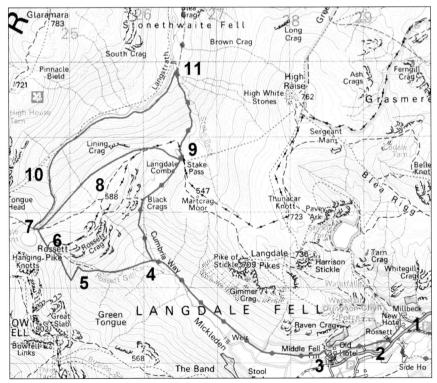

Map 60: Langdale to Langstrath.

Old Hotel. The higher one forms part of the Cumbria Way and leaves towards the bottom of the car park and ends above the Old Hotel. There is then a short descent to the valley floor path. The other path (2) leaves a little further down the car park, is rather less undulating and ends up near to the car park at the Old Hotel. Another choice is just to walk along the road and turn right to the Old Hotel.

The wide and clear valley floor path starts just behind the western end of the Old Hotel (3). This path is pretty much flat all the way to the head of the Langdale Valley. This is one of the most well-known and heavily-walked valleys in the Lake District with famous mountains rising up spectacularly on both sides. After about three kilometres the path divides (4) with the right-hand path heading off to Stake Pass. This is the route back (or there if you prefer). The left branch heads for the route up Rossett Gill. Two paths up Rossett Gill are shown on the OS map. One goes straight up, the other zigzagging to the left. By far the better choice is the one zigzagging to the left (5). Both Hindle and Wainwright describe another path which arises before the start of the branch to Stake Pass and goes to the left of the other routes, much more on the side of Bow Fell. This is almost certainly the old packhorse route but has become unused and is now difficult to follow and is not shown on the OS map. Bits of it can still be seen, particularly when coming down Stake Pass.

From the top of Rossett Gill Pass (6) go down along the packhorse route, towards Sty Head and Wasdale, which goes to the right of Angle Tarn. At the outlet of the tarn (7), Angletarn Gill, there are two paths leaving to the right. The first (8) is just before the gill, and goes along the flank of Rossett Pike to the top of Stake Pass (9) and is a perfectly reasonable way back. This path is very wet in places and often entails a detour but the compensation is that little height is gained or lost.

The second path (10), just after the gill, follows it down to the floor of Langstrath. This may have been one of the packhorse routes to Rosthwaite from Eskdale and Ore gap. On the floor of the valley, where Langstrath Beck is formed from Allencraggs Gill and Angletarn Gill, keep to the path on its right bank. Follow the beck around until it joins Stake Beck then turn right (11) and climb up the zigzags to Stake Pass. Cross the wide pass (9), at about 480 metres, and descend the zigzags on the far side to regain the floor of the Langdale Valley. The path is easy to see and follow all the way over the pass. It just remains to walk along the Langdale Valley to where you left your car. The longer route is about twelve kilometres and takes three to four hours.

8) MARDALE HEAD TO KENTMERE AND SADGILL (Sadgill Bridge)
(see also Nan Bield, Gatescarth Pass, short walk 5 and circular walk 9)
This walk starts at the small car park at Mardale Head (1). There is also some limited parking alongside the road but, if you want to avoid this, it is as well to arrive early. If the weather has been dry, try to spot the walls leading into the lost village of Mardale Green. The village buildings were demolished by Manchester Corporation in order that the valley could be flooded to a greater depth to provide the city with water. The Act of Parliament to create the reservoir was passed in 1919 and the building of the dam was started in 1929. There was little local resistance other than from the village children who used to follow the surveyors pulling out and throwing away their wooden marker pegs. The inhabitants were tenants and received no compensation.

The village church had its last service in 1935 after which the buildings were dynamited to prevent any going back. It was an act of civic arrogance that these days seems almost inconceivable outside a totalitarian state. On the other hand we all need a secure supply of water but perhaps a less picturesque spot could have been found. Nevertheless it happened and the dam that produced the flood can be seen at the north-eastern end of Haweswater. It was the first hollow, buttress dam in the world. It is made of concrete and has 24 huge arches inside and 44 buttresses outside.

Downstream of the dam is what remains of the buildings that housed the temporary workers. This was the model village of Burnbanks which had 66 bungalows made of iron-framed concrete panels, a canteen, shops and

Plate 32: Chapel Bridge, 1984 (Dr. Brumhead, Carlisle Library)

other facilities. After the dam was completed in 1940 many workers and their families stayed on but the buildings gradually became more and more fun down. In 2004-5 the eighteen surviving buildings were rebuilt and now form a small community. Sarah Hall wrote a novel called *Haweswater* which was set in Mardale at the time of the building of the dam.

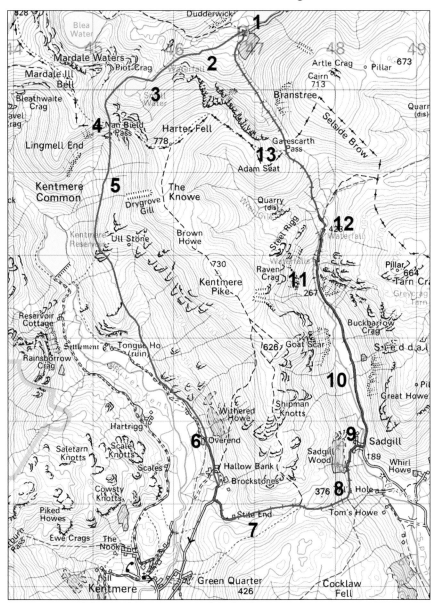

Map 61: Mardale Head, Kentmere and Sadgill.

Mardale had two stone-arch bridges, Chapel Bridge over Mardale Beck in the centre of the village and Arnold Bridge further east over Hopgill Beck. Both occasionally reappear in severe droughts providing an illustration of the powers of endurance of stone arches. Riggindale Bridge, a metal-beam bridge to the west of the village, was dismantled and re-erected in Wet Sleddale. As well as Mardale Green another hamlet, called Measand, was inundated and nothing of it remains other than the school which was transplanted down the valley to Walmgate Head and is now a private house. Measand was on the road that ran down the west side of Haweswater at a point called The Straits, where the old Haweswater narrowed almost to the point of being divided in two, rather like Thirlmere, another lake turned reservoir. Measand had an arched bridge, which has not been seen since the reservoir filled, but a greater claim to fame is that it had the first library where books were lent out free of charge.

Leave the car park and head south-west, along the middle of the three paths (2) towards Small Water with Small Water Beck to the right. Climb up to the tarn (3) and cross its outlet and go past the slate shelters by the path. The route then climbs more steeply on zigzags to the top of the pass (4) where there is another shelter. Continue over the pass and down the zigzags to reach a clear path (5) to Overend in the Kentmere Valley. At Overend fork left along the upper of the two paths (6). Shortly afterwards this becomes a tarmac road. After about 200 metres turn left off this road and through a gate onto a rough track with stone walls on each side and head east up the hill past Stile End (7). This is an old drovers' road which goes over a low pass to Sadgill in the Longsleddale Valley. It is easy to follow to the top. Not long after the descent starts, turn left (8) through a gateway and go down a rough stony path heading north with Sadgill Wood in front and to the left. Almost at the end of this track there is a farm on the right and it then opens up and Sadgill packhorse bridge (9) becomes visible. The bridge is a genuine packhorse bridge although it has been widened. Go over the bridge and turn left along the road going north up the valley (10).

The road to the right, leading down the valley, was also a packhorse route to and from Kendal. The Sprint, which is a fair-sized river at this point, is to the left as you go up the valley. At first there are walled fields in the valley bottom but these stop at about the level of Galeforth Brow. Shortly after this there is what looks like a failed dam across the valley floor. These are the remains of a nineteenth century scheme to make a reservoir to provide water power for the mills downstream. The road itself is a quarry road to the now-disused Wrengill Quarry at the top of Gatescarth Pass but it was probably built on top of the existing packhorse route. The road ascends fairly steeply towards the end of the valley (11) with waterfalls to the left and has a rough, made-up, stone surface which no doubt helped the quarry horses. After the waterfall is passed the route flattens and crosses a small stone bridge.

The path continues to be obvious and fairly flat. A little further on the path to Mosedale, and thence to Swindale and Wet Sleddale, branches off almost at a right angle (12). To the left and further up the mountain are the remains of Wrengill Quarry. This was a slate quarry and, according to Wainwright, was last worked by Italian prisoners of war. Considerable signs of its existence remain with a quarry area, pipes, an old railway embankment and some ruined buildings.

Gatescarth Pass lies ahead and up a steep but clear path. Eventually, and with some relief, the summit (at 594 metres) (13) is reached and the stony and twisting path down to Mardale Head comes into sight. It is an easy descent along stony zigzags to the car park with rewarding views of Haweswater and, ultimately, a well-earned rest. There are no buildings here so any refreshment, equally well-earned, must have been thought about in advance and stashed in the car. The walk is about sixteen kilometres long and takes approximately five hours.

9) MARDALE HEAD TO MOSEDALE AND SWINDALE (no bridges)
(see also Gatescarth Pass, Mardale Corpse Road and circular walk 8)
This is a packhorses route without bridges. It starts at the Mardale Head car park (1) and heads up the steep but zigzagged path (2) to Gatescarth Pass. Alternatively start at the smaller car park (11) at the foot of the Old Corpse Road opposite The Rigg and walk down the road or along the lake shore path (12) to the Mardale Head car park. From here, go through the gate at the end of the road and take the path on the left with Gatescarth Beck to the left. Climb up the zigzags to the top of the pass (3).

By this time Haweswater and its valley have disappeared but new views are opening up down Longsleddale. Continue along the clear path and descend to Brownehowe Bottom (4) with the quarry workings to your right. This path is better engineered than the uphill part, perhaps a legacy of the quarry. Unfortunately this has allowed it to be used as a race track by cyclists. These are not the typical mountain cyclists, who cause little offence, but a more-heavily-helmeted set of thrill seekers who risk brain and bone as they hurtle down the bends. And not just their brains and bones but also those of any walker unfortunate enough to meet them unexpectedly around a corner. As well as cyclists I have also met recreational Land Rovers struggling over the pass, in spite of the way being blocked by gates with combination locks.

Towards the bottom of the descent there is a path off to the right

heading in the direction of the old workings of Wrengill Quarry (5).
Quarry explorers will want to see the rusting pipeline that carried water
from Wren Gill down the hillside to be used in the works. The pipeline
starts at the end of a short channel branching off from the gill. There are
several ruined slate buildings scattered around, one containing a rusting
six cylinder engine, and some steep drops and fast-moving water. From the
quarry there is a path down to Brownehowe Bottom.

Returning from the quarry, or more sensibly never having been distract-
ed in the first place, turn left (4) from the main path just after some sheep
folds by a sign post saying 'Public Footpath to Swindale Head 3½ miles,
Wet Sleddale 5 miles.' There is a stream to cross almost immediately and
this is a sign of things to come. The next few kilometres can be very wet in
places, although not impassable. This is probably a walk best done after a
period of dry weather which will also allow a better chance of seeing the
walls and roads of Mardale Green as the level of the reservoir goes down.

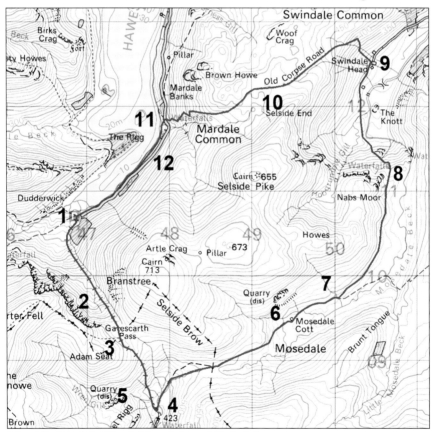

Map 62: Mardale Head, Mosedale and Swindale.

The path is fairly obvious and rises gently only to descend again towards Mosedale, the 'valley with the bog,' certainly that. This is dreary countryside with little to recommend it apart from solitude. Shortly after reaching the top of the slope Mosedale Cottage (6) comes into view with extensive spoil heaps above it. Like the Black Sail Hut and Skiddaw House this is one of the Lake District's more remote dwellings. It is now maintained by the Mountain Bothy Association and although a little spartan it is no doubt a welcome refuge from the cold, dark and wet in such an empty and desolate place.

A short distance beyond the bothy is a ford which can require some ingenuity to cross with dry feet. Having done this, continue on the path until the last enclosure is passed and the path divides (7). The right-hand branch goes to Wet Sleddale and the left to Swindale Head. Follow the latter as it contours around keeping Mosedale Beck below and to the right. Eventually, and, no surprise this, after several wet patches, the top of the Swindale Valley is reached (8). To the right of the path are some impressive waterfalls called 'The Forces' but these are not visible from the path and a detour has to be made to see them. This would not have been considered by the packhorse men but should you wish to visit there is a narrow path off to the right. The falls are in several stages with deep pools beneath them and a somewhat precarious path descends alongside. Alternatively take the packhorse route as it zigzags down to Swindale.

On the floor of the valley there is a wide and clear path that winds its way around the drumlins and then becomes enclosed by stone walls. Continue along this path, past a stone barn on the right, until the farmhouse at Swindale Head (9) is reached. This is where the tarmac road that runs along the valley floor starts. Turn left here and climb steeply on the Old Corpse Road (sign-posted) towards Mardale. This becomes less steep as it curves to head south west and then over Mardale Common (10) where the path is marked with posts. In due course there are magnificent views of Haweswater and the mountains and valleys on its far side. Go past some ruined stone buildings and after a short descent on some zigzags the road (11) appears and your car is either there or a little further up the valley.

If your car is at Mardale Head you can walk along the road or take the lake shore path (12). This is sign-posted just across the road. It is a narrow and undulating path with frequent manhole covers to remind you that this is no ordinary lake. The first part of the path is close to, and heads in the direction of, the now-submerged Mardale Green, the "Atlantis of the Lake District." It is a little disturbing to think of the places that were, and the lives that were led, as one walks past the dark waters of the reservoir. The route, without detours, is between thirteen and fourteen kilometres and takes about five hours.

10) SEATHWAITE TO STONETHWAITE VIA LANGSTRATH
(Stockley Bridge)
(see also Esk Hause, Ore Gap, Sty Head Pass and circular walks 4, 5 and 11)
One of the attractions of this walk is that there is almost unlimited parking
(1) on the verge along the road to Seathwaite Farm. Not only that but the
farm offers refreshments as well. Go straight through the farm, ignoring
the path on the right between some farm buildings, and head off towards
the hills in front of you (2). The path is wide and obvious and fairly flat as

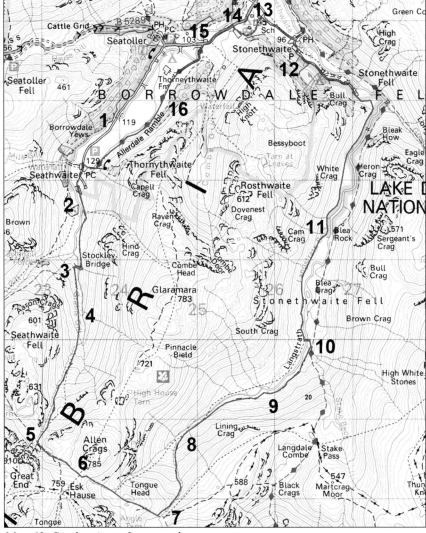

Map 63: Seathwaite to Langstrath.

it heads south up the valley with the river on the right. After about one kilometre the path crosses Stockley Bridge (3), a genuine, albeit rebuilt, packhorse bridge. Immediately after the bridge take the path (4) to the left with Grains Gill on your left and start to climb up the valley. The path is a good one and dry for the most part although rocky in places.

Half way up, the path crosses Ruddy Gill on a wooden bridge. It continues to climb with the deep Ruddy Gorge to the right. Eventually the top is reached and the great highway (5) between Sty Head and the Langdale valley comes into view. After dropping down a little and crossing the stream turn left on the new path and climb up to the col (6) between Esk Hause and Allen Crags. Continue on and descend to Angle Tarn. Turn left on a path (7) just before the stream draining the tarn and descend towards Langstrath. An alternative path is shown on the OS map going down beside Allencrags Gill between Allen Crags and Tongue Head. This is also the path that is indicated in Hindle's book but I have never been able to find it and the area seems too steep for a packhorse route. Perhaps it was the original route and has fallen into disuse and disappeared. For packhorse trains coming over Ore Gap from Eskdale and going to Borrowdale via Langstrath the Angle Tarn route would have been easier.

The Angle Tarn path descends alongside Angletarn Gill which joins Allencrags Gill where the gradient becomes much less steep (8). Continue along the path (9) on the right (east) side of the river, now called Langstrath Beck. Further on a path appears on the far side of the river. Hindle shows the packhorse route to be on the left bank but it is a matter of choice when to cross over. Perhaps it is easiest at the bridge (10) just after Stake Beck joins. It is then a pleasant and easy walk along the valley floor to Stonethwaite. About halfway along the valley the river forms a deep pool with steep rocky sides called Blackmoss Pot (11). After this the river is wider and becomes even wider after it is joined by Greenup Gill. The valley turns to the left here and shortly afterwards the small village of Stonethwaite (12) comes into view. You have a choice here of a drink at the pub or a cup of tea at one of the cottages a little further on.

Go through the village and out onto the tarmac road leading to Rosthwaite. Turn left on the road just after the school (13) and go past the church, through a farm yard and across some fields to join the main Borrowdale Valley road (14). Turn left on the road and after a short distance turn left again at Strands Bridge (15) and follow the path (16) to Seathwaite on the opposite side of the valley to the road leading to the farm where you hope your car is still parked. You can cross back to your car at the farm. Depending on where you have left your car it might be quicker to keep to the valley road and approach the parking area from the opposite direction.

The walk is about eighteen kilometres long and takes five or six hours.

11) SEATHWAITE TO WASDALE HEAD AND ON TO HONISTER
(Stockley Bridge and Wasdale Head Bridge)
(see also Burn Moor, Moses Trod and Sty Head Pass and circular walks 2, 5 and 10)

As on the previous walk, leave your car at Seathwaite (1) and amble south along the valley floor to Stockley Bridge (2). This time go straight ahead after crossing the bridge and climb the rocky path (3) with Styhead Gill to the right and a long way below. As you gradually get higher and turn to the left, the route gets closer to the river and then crosses it on a wooden bridge (4). Continue on with Green Gable on your right and pass Styhead Tarn on the left until Sty Head Pass (5) is reached with the mountain rescue box clearly visible.

Go to the left of the box and about 50 metres further on the old packhorse route (6) leaves on the left, moving away from the usual walkers' path to Wasdale Head. Its start is not obvious, although there is a small cairn, and it begins in a shallow, grassy, v-shaped hollow and then

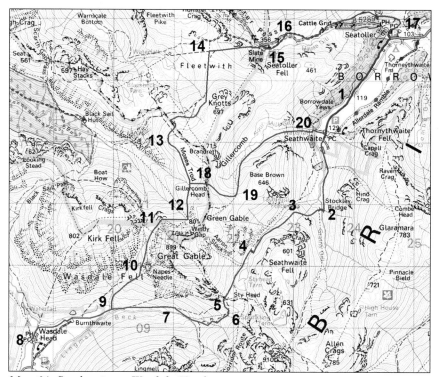

Map 64: Seathwaite to Wasdale Head.

descends on more-obvious zigzags to cross Spouthead Gill. It crosses back further down (7) and then stays close to the right bank of the river as it descends to Wasdale Head (8) and the delightful Wasdale Head Bridge. A suitable place for lunch.

There are various choices on the way back. The easiest is just to turn around and retrace your steps. More of a challenge is to use a path called Moses Trod for at least part of the way back. If you decide to be challenged, leave Wasdale Head the way you came but fork to the left (9) just after the long wooden footbridge with the single stone pier, to go north up the side of Great Gable with Gable Beck on the left. This is something of a slog but is rewarded by rearward views over Wasdale Head and Wast Water when you stop to get your breath back. Well up the mountain and into the screes, fork left (10) and ascend more gently around the side of Gable. Moses Trod stays above the path to Beck Head to reach the lip (11) of the Ennerdale Valley. Going over this you can then descend into the top of the Ennerdale Valley at Stone Cove and then up the other side (12) towards Honister. Continue on this path which rises slowly to go over the other lip of the Ennerdale valley. It crosses a fence on a stile to join the path coming down from Brandreth and Green Gable and then contours around (13) all the way to the old drum house (14) on the dismantled tramway which descends almost to the slate works at Honister Pass (15). There is tea at the slate works, should you need it, and a glimpse of the slate industry.

Honister Pass was on a packhorse route from Buttermere to Rosthwaite but now has a motor road crossing it. The descent to Seatoller can be made much more interesting by avoiding the tarmac road and following the old toll road (16), built by the quarry company, shown on the OS map as a dashed double line. This leaves the bottom of the lower car park at the slate works, descends gradually, then crosses the motor road and continues down on the far side, later on turning right to share the road again for a short distance. As it moves away from the road again it stays higher up the valley side than the road and Hause Gill, and then turns back on itself and descends to join the road at Seatoller, another place for tea. The road to Seathwaite is a little further on and to the right (17). The whole walk is about twenty kilometres and takes about seven hours.

A shorter alternative, although not on a packhorse route, is to turn right (18) off Moses Trod as it ascends the side of Ennerdale and go over Gillercombe Head and then drop down to join the path (19) going along Gillercombe from Green Gable. This involves a short length of off-path bushwhacking so some care is needed. The Gillercombe path goes down to Seathwaite alongside Sourmilk Gill and over the Seathwaite Slabs (20). This means doing some mild scrambling which may not be to everyone's taste but really is not difficult. The path leads to the centre of the farm at Seathwaite with tea and cakes.

12) STONETHWAITE TO GREENUP EDGE AND WATENDLATH
 (Watendlath Bridge)
(see also Greenup Edge, Watendlath, circular walk 6 and short walk 10)
The link between the two packhorse routes in this walk goes over Ullscarf which is generally taken to be the most central fell in the Lake District. Wainwright describes the summit as a "cheerless place" with "no vestige of shelter." It is certainly pretty unremarkable as summits go, indeed it would be easy to miss were it not for its cairn with a fence post poking out

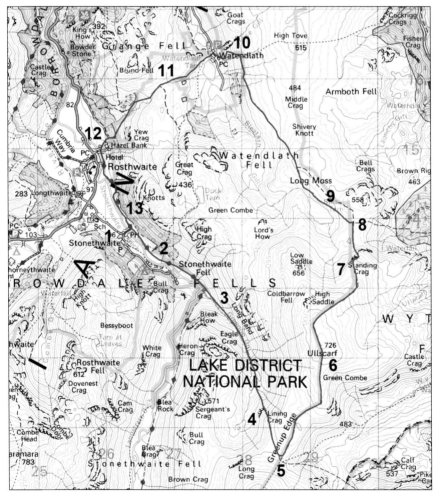

Map 65: Stonethwaite to Greenup Edge and Watendlath.

of it. Nevertheless the path over it makes a useful and wild link between
two of the best packhorse routes in the Lake District. After the ascent to
Lining Crag, on the way to Greenup Edge, much of the ground is wet and
the walk is probably best done after a dry period.

A convenient place to start is the lovely village of Stonethwaite ("the
stony clearing") (1) towards the end of the Borrowdale Valley. There is limited parking in the village and at one or two places along the road approaching it. If parking is a problem the walk can just as easily be started at
Rosthwaite where there is more space in an official car park and also next
to the Scafell Hotel. From Rosthwaite cross the bridge over Stonethwaite
Beck, turn right at the signpost to Stonethwaite and walk along the path
(13) beside the river to Stonethwaite. Similarly, starting from Stonethwaite
cross the bridge in the village and turn right onto the same path (2), part of
the Cumbria Way, heading south east towards the valley of Langstrath.
After a kilometre, alongside Smithymire Island, take the left fork (3) and
start to climb up towards Greenup Edge along a clear, stony path with
Greenup Gill on the right. The path crosses several small streams, none of
which poses a problem, and gradually gains height with Lining Crag (4)
appearing and disappearing ahead as the path rises and then flattens. The
crag looks unassailable from the front and to the right but the path takes a
set of zigzags to the left and the top is soon reached. Below and to the right,
where most of Greenup Gill originates, is an area full of drumlins. Once on
top of the crag most of the climb has been done and it is worth resting for
a few moments to admire the view down the valley.

The path continues up towards the pass but becomes much wetter and
many small detours may be needed. Towards the top of the pass turn left
(5) and head roughly north on a narrow path which meanders alongside the
remains of an iron fence. This area is a watershed between the Borrowdale
and Thirlmere valleys and much of it is wet underfoot as well as having
streams and small tarns. The path swings more to the east for a time but
then goes north again to reach the summit of Ullscarf (6) at 726 metres.
The meaning of Ullscarf is obscure but "Wolf's gap" is suggested by
Whaley. It would be more convincing if there were a gap.

Although the summit is insignificant, the views are anything but, with
Hevellyn and Fairfield to the east, Skiddaw to the north, Pillar and the
Gables to the west and Coniston Old Man to the south; almost a Full
House. At least I think there is. In the interests of ethical writing I must
make a small confession here. When I first did this walk the top link was
covered in mist. Not so much that navigation was a problem but enough to
block the distant views. I repeated the walk a few weeks later with the
express purpose of seeing the view for myself. Armed with a good weath-

er forecast and with the ridge clearly in view as I climbed up towards Greenup Edge, I reached the top only to find the mist closing in. The only difference this time was that the mist was thicker and I had to navigate the length of the ridge with a compass, although the fence posts helped. But Wainwright says the above, and more, are all visible and you can't do better than that.

After taking in the view, if there is one, continue more or less straight on, following the line of intermittent, rusting fence posts. A few hundred metres further on there is a wire fence and the path moves to the right and descends gently beside it. After about half a kilometre the path turns to the north again and shortly afterwards goes to the right of Standing Crag (7) to reach the pass between Ullscarf and Armboth Fell. Continue alongside the fence and turn left through the second gate (8) to join the packhorse route from Wythburn to Watendlath.

The path towards Watendlath descends gradually along wet, at times very wet, ground on the right (9) of Blea Tarn. Eventually Watendlath Tarn appears below and a little to the left. Almost level with Watendlath the path turns sharply to the left (10) and descends on made-up zigzags to reach the hamlet which has a welcome tea shop. There is usually a small crowd of people admiring the delightful setting with its tarn, vernacular buildings and, of course, its packhorse bridge. There are three farms, Stepps End, Fold Head and Caffel How, all owned by the National Trust, as is the tarn. The area was once part of the estates of Furness Abbey. It was the fictional home of Hugh Walpole's Judith Paris whose name appears on a stone sign on the house next to the tea shop.

Cross the bridge over the outlet to the tarn and shortly afterwards take the right fork to climb up to Puddingstone Bank (11) on a wide path, also a packhorse route. At this stage in the walk a climb is not necessarily very welcome but it is short and not very steep and pretty soon you are walking along the longer, and rockier, descent towards Rosthwaite and the Borrowdale Valley. Assuming your car is in Stonethwaite, turn left at the bottom of the descent at the signpost (12), just before the bridge, and walk the kilometre or so on the path (13) to Stonethwaite. There is an alternative path a little higher up, also signposted, which joins the valley path about half way to Stonethwaite. Rosthwaite and Stonethwaite both have tea shops. The walk is about sixteen kilometres long and takes approximately six hours.

6: STRUCTURES

The next two chapters discuss the technology of bridges and their construction in more detail than in chapter one. Inevitably some mathematics creeps in but it is mainly a qualitative account. The maths and more technical sections are in italics. Both of these chapters can be safely omitted by those who just want to enjoy the packhorse bridges and their connecting paths and are only included for people who may wish to know more about bridges.

A bridge is a structure, which is technically a system for transferring loads from one place to another, and a structure has to resist the forces it is exposed to. Bridges are exposed to forces which have three origins:- the dead load (the weight of the bridge itself), the live load (the weight of the traffic passing over it) and the environmental load (e.g. wind and river water pushing on it). The success and longevity of a bridge is a measure of how well it withstands these forces.

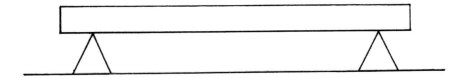

Fig. 5: A simply-supported beam, unloaded

There are three basic types of bridge: beam, arch and suspension. A beam is a structural member subject to bending when loaded, such as a plank. Usually the beam is horizontal and supported at two or more points and the load presses vertically downwards. The simplest situation is the 'simply-supported beam' shown above. (Strictly speaking the beam is attached by a hinge at one end and supported by a roller at the other but for simplicity it is shown here supported on knife-edge trestles.) The live and dead loads of a beam pass along its length and then vertically downwards into its supports at each end. There is no sideways thrust on the supports. This leads to the idea of the 'line of force or thrust'. This is an imaginary line passing through a structure, from top to bottom, which defines the positions and directions at which the thrust can be considered to be acting at each successive joint.*

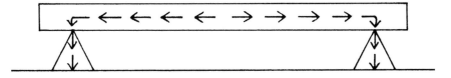

Fig. 6: The line of thrust in a simply supported beam

For an unloaded horizontal uniform beam the downwards thrust on each support is the weight of the beam (mass x acceleration due to gravity), divided equally between the two supports.

$$V = \frac{M L g}{2}$$

where V = *vertical thrust downwards*
          M = *mass per unit length of the beam*
          L = *length of the beam*
          g = *acceleration due to gravity*

Hence a uniform beam twice as long produces twice the downwards thrust on its supports. Loading the beam obviously increases the downwards force on the supports, its distribution between the two supports depending on the position of the load.

An irascible man called Robert Hooke showed that the stretching of a material or the deflection of a structure is proportional to the applied load.** So doubling the load on a structure produces twice the deflection. Up to a point the material or structure will return to its original length or shape when the load is removed i.e. it behaves elastically. Beyond this 'elastic limit' some permanent change takes place. The 'worst case' for this beam is when the live load is at the point midway between the two end

---

*The concept of the line of thrust is thought to have originated with the eighteenth century French physicist Charles Coulomb from his work on retaining walls. In a vertical wall the line of thrust goes straight down the middle. As long as it stays in the middle third the wall will remain stable. If the wall has a sideways thrust added to it, perhaps from a heavy sloping roof or the weight of earth pushing on a retaining wall, the line may move away from the middle third causing cracks to appear on the opposite side. If the move is large enough the wall will collapse. This has relevance for masonry abutments, piers and arches.
** 'As the extension so the force.' It became known as Hooke's Law and was published by him in 1679 as a Latin anagram. Presumably accessibility was less of an issue then.

supports. This is the time when that particular load will produce the biggest downward deflection and the most likely time that the beam will fail. Also the longer the beam the greater the deflection. Perhaps surprisingly, doubling the length of a beam increases the deflection of the beam under the same load by a factor of eight, unless its elastic limit is exceeded, in which case it will be more. Other factors are the stiffness of the material making up the beam (its Young's Modulus) and its cross-sectional shape.

$$\Delta = \frac{M \, g \, L^3}{48 \, E \, I}$$

where Δ = *maximum deflection of the beam at its mid point*
M = *mass per unit length of the beam*
g = *acceleration due to gravity*
L = *length of the beam between supports*
E = *Young's Modulus*
I = *a constant dependent on the cross-sectional shape of the beam (the second moment of area of cross-section about the neutral axis)*

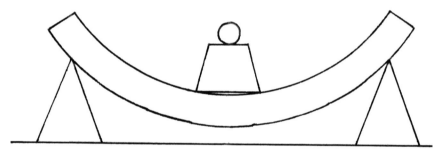

Fig. 7: A loaded beam with a central downward deflection

When the beam is loaded at its midpoint the top surface of the beam is shortened (i.e. it is in compression) and the bottom surface is stretched (i.e. it is in tension). If you find this difficult to visualise, imagine a beam made of sponge rubber and suppose that the beam is short enough and the sponge stiff enough to remain horizontal when it is unloaded and supported at each end. Suppose that lines are painted across the width of the beam equal distances apart, top and bottom, and joined at the edges. When the beam is unloaded the lines stay equal distances apart.

When the beam is loaded the lines on top move closer together (i.e. the material between the lines is compressed) and those below move apart. An

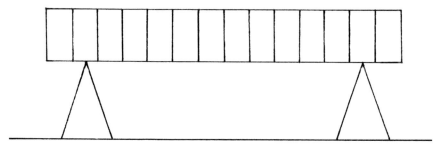

Fig. 8: An unloaded beam with lines as described above.

imaginary line running equidistant between the top and bottom (called the 'neutral axis') stays the same length i.e. it is neither in tension nor compression.

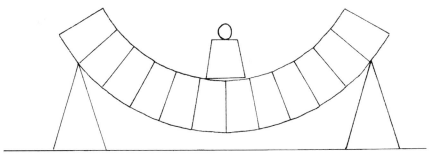

Fig. 9: A beam under load at its centre with lines as described above.

Most types of wood are a little stronger in tension than in compression so if a beam is made of wood it will usually fail in compression on its top surface, producing creases at right angles to the length of the beam. The reason that this beam would make quite a successful bridge is that wood is generally strong enough not to fail under reasonable loads, always provided that the span is not excessive and the wood is of reasonable thickness and quality. The beam will certainly deflect downwards with the load but will tend to return to its previous state when the load is removed i.e. it is elastic. Most successful structures have a measure of elasticity. Whole tree trunks are even stronger than planks but of course are less practical as bridge surfaces.

If the beam ends are clamped (i.e. cannot rotate upwards) then a different situation develops with loading. The beam deflects downwards with three curves and two points of inflection (points at which the curve changes direction). Clamped beams are more efficient than simply supported beams and the same beam can carry one and a half times the load

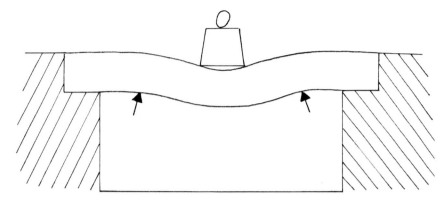

Fig. 10: A beam fixed at each end and under load showing points of inflection

while deflecting only a fifth as much. Wood is still a suitable material for this type of beam.

If these beams were to be made of stone, however, the story would be different. Stone is strong in compression but weak in tension. So a stone beam would break, quite easily, at its bottom surface.

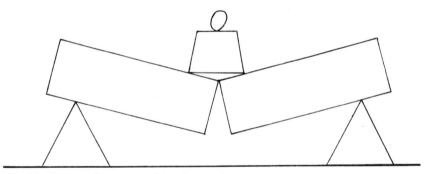

Fig. 11: A stone beam cracking in tension

To be safe under load any stone beam has to be relatively short and massive. Hence most stone-beam clapper bridges are over small streams, such as the one over Cawdale Beck. Anything wider needs multiple spans, such as the one at Troutbeck Park, with all the problems that building supporting piers can bring. Near Dulverton in Somerset there is an ancient clapper bridge 55 metres long with seventeen spans.

Concrete has the same limitations as stone but can be strengthened, or reinforced, by incorporating steel rods. As the concrete is weakest in tension the rods are best placed close to the bottom of the beam, although it is then important to get the beam the right way up. An alternative is to put the concrete into compression before it is loaded, for example by tensioning the steel rods while they are being covered with the concrete, anchoring the rods to the concrete and then releasing the tension as the concrete cures. The parts of the beam that would have been put into tension when loaded now just have less compression and still function well. Other parts are even more in compression but this can be tolerated. The concrete also protects the rods from corrosion. Another variation is post-tensioning where cables are threaded through ducts in the concrete, then stretched and anchored. Pre-stressed concrete has been the darling of post-war bridge construction as it is versatile, relatively cheap and makes strong beams. In most circumstances it is an acceptable substitute for steel beams.

For a given span and beam thickness, wood is a much better choice for a simple beam bridge than stone. Clearly there are limits to the size of span, even for a wooden beam bridge, and for wide rivers the beams have to be supported at intervals along their lengths. Although some early railway bridges, particularly in America but also in Britain, had wooden supporting towers, called trestles, nearly all supporting piers are made of masonry to avoid rotting and it is likely that most of the early wooden Lake District bridges were the same. As the load on the piers would be pushing downwards the masonry would be happily in compression. Piers raise all sorts of other problems, such as how you build them in the middle of rivers and how they fail as the river bed is removed by the eddies they cause (see chapter 7), but most of these can be overcome by effort and ingenuity.

Wooden bridges have to be rebuilt at intervals and it is natural that stone would be preferred for its longevity if nothing else. Stone and brick are excellent building materials provided that they are kept in compression and not exposed to much tension. As we have already seen the easiest way of doing this is to use an arch which is a structure almost entirely in compression. Of course an arch can be made of other materials as long as they are strong in compression, such as cast iron in the Iron Bridge at Coalbrookdale in Shropshire, built in 1779, or the many steel arches. Masonry arches will be considered in more detail in the next chapter.

The cross-sectional shape of a beam can be designed to give it the greatest possible strength per unit mass. We said above that a loaded horizontal beam simply supported at each end is in compression along its top surface and in tension along its bottom surface. Along its middle it is in neither tension nor compression and serves to connect the top and bottom parts and to deal with the shear, or sliding, forces so generated. These are much less than the compression and tension and it is therefore more efficient to make the shape of the girder so that it is thick at the top and bottom, the flanges,

and thin in the middle, the web. This accounts for the typical 'I' shaped
girder. For small spans this is all that is necessary. The old Penrith to
Cockermouth railway had several girder bridges, some of whose masonry
abutments can still be seen. Early railway girder bridges were made from
wrought iron or the more-suspect, but cheaper, cast iron. Later ones were
made from steel.

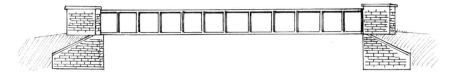

Fig. 12: A steel girder (or beam) bridge.

Bigger spans need more complicated solutions. One weakness of the 'I'
girder is that it can twist. A shape better able to resist twisting is a box girder which has two webs. Many modern road bridges are made from steel or
pre-stressed concrete box girders.

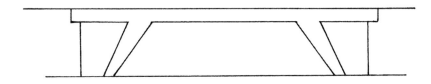

Fig. 13: A rigid-frame bridge.

One solution to bridging large gaps is the rigid frame bridge where the
supports are part of the structure of the platform and lean out from the
banks towards the centre of the bridge removing the necessity for building
piers in the river bed.

Another option is to provide support from above with a steel arch. Steel
is a suitable material from which to build an arch as it is about as strong in
compression as it is in tension, although it can buckle in compression and
fail at the points of connection when used in tension, as in the Clyde Arc
in January 2008; bridge failures are not always things of the distant past.
The arch is usually split length-wise into two parallel arches supporting
the platform in between them with vertical steel tension members. The
arch itself can be anchored at each end into natural rock or masonry abutments or it can be anchored to itself using steel tension girders running
horizontally along the length of the bridge platform, a so-called tied-arch

Plate 33: Overline erect tied-arch bridge on the disused Penrith to Cockermouth railway.

bridge. This was quite often used in railway bridging as it could just be laid on top of the reinforced river banks. Three can be seen on the disused Penrith to Cockermouth railway between Thelkeld and Keswick starting at NY313248 (there is a convenient parking area on the road above) and walking towards Keswick.

As well as these three skewed, but otherwise conventional, erect over-line tied arches there are also three less-conventional, underline inverted tied-arches. When it is inverted the arch is in tension rather than in compression and the vertical supports are in compression. These bridges were designed between 1862 and 1864 by Thomas Bouch, better known for designing the ill-fated Tay Bridge, and were made from wrought iron. It was said that Bouch preferred the inverted arch although it is hard to see why with the extra strain put on the fastenings. (One of my friends wondered if the workmen just had the plans upside down.) Each had to be significantly strengthened with a massive steel horizontal girder, almost as deep as the arch itself, just below the platform in the 1920s and 30s to deal with heavier locomotives. The erect arches faired better but still needed some bracing at the tops and sides of the arches.

The carriageway can be somewhere between the top and bottom of the arch, such as in the Tyne Bridge in Newcastle. In this case the vertical supporting steels are in tension if they are above the carriageway or in

Plate 34: Underline inverted tied-arch bridge on the disused Penrith to Cockermouth railway.

compression if they are below. Large steel arches are usually built using creeper cranes at the ends of each incomplete arch with cables anchored on each bank holding back the arches. Tied arches can be prefabricated and just lifted into position.

A less elegant, but possibly cheaper, solution is to use a truss. These originated as wooden structures in Germany in the fifteenth century, often covered to protect the wood from the elements. They evolved into a mixture of wood and iron and eventually became all steel. A truss is, in effect, a big beam, made up of shorter lengths of steel fastened together in such a way as to make a strong and rigid supporting structure. "All exploit the

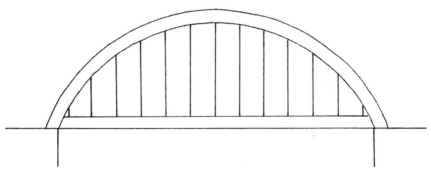

Fig. 14: A tied-arch bridge

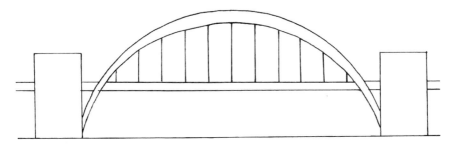

Fig. 15: Steel arch bridge with carriageway in the centre of the arch

rigidity of the triangle and balance compressive and tensile forces to achieve structural purpose" (Brown). To which might be added, "with variable degrees of success." In the 1870s, in the United States, wood and iron truss bridges were collapsing at the rate of 40 per year, one for every four built, often from problems with the fixings at their many joints.

The roadway or railway can be above, below or somewhere along the middle of the truss. There are many different types, often named after their inventors. The Warren truss just has diagonal members for short spans but vertical members are added for longer ones. In the Pratt truss the diagonal members all slant down towards the centre of the span. The top and bottom horizontal members behave like any other beam under load, the top ones in compression and the bottom ones in tension. Any vertical members are in tension if the roadway is along the bottom of the truss and in compression if it is along the top. The diagonals vary according to their positions and the type of truss. Large steel arch bridges are often made with a curved truss forming the arch such as in the Tyne Bridge.

You can see a truss bridge over the river Eden on the road between Alston and Penrith (A 686) at Langwathby in Cumbria. It is a Callender-Hamilton Bridge, put in place in 1968 as a 'temporary measure' to replace a 300-year-old sandstone bridge with three arches, which had been washed

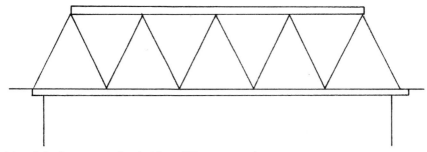

Fig. 16: A truss girder bridge (Warren type).

away by floods. A. M. Hamilton was a New Zealander who was the principle engineer of the road that bore his name in Iraqi Kurdistan. Building
this road convinced him of the need for a robust, portable and adaptable
bridge that could be easily transported and erected in difficult terrain. The
Callender part came from the engineering company British Insulated
Callenders Cables which manufactured it. Although it may have been a
quick and practical solution to this particular crossing, the bridge at
Langwathby has only a single carriageway and it would be difficult to call
it beautiful. A wider, multi-arched bridge, made from the local red sandstone, would be a more elegant solution. In fact, rather like the one it
replaced.

Truss bridges are much favoured by the military as they can be easily
transported in bits, quickly assembled on one bank and then pushed across
the river in sections. The design of the Callender-Hamilton Bridge preced-
ed another truss bridge, the more famous Bailey Bridge, which infringed
its patent leading to a successful claim to the Royal Commission for
Awards to Inventors. Sir Donald Bailey was a civil engineer at the War
Office during the Second World War whose hobby was making model
bridges. One of these impressed his superiors enough for it to be put into
production. It was first used in Italy in 1943 and by the end of the war several thousand had been used by the Allied armies. One can be seen crossing the river near the entrance to Allen Banks, an area of woodland owned

Plate 35: A temporary Bailey Bridge in the Northumberland Cheviots.

by the National Trust along the River Allen in Northumberland. Like the bridge at Langwathby, it is more a thing of utility than beauty. The Bailey Bridge could be made as long and as strong as necessary by just adding more parts. As a demonstration of its versitility one was employed as a rocket launching tower in Australia.

Another type of bridge is based on the cantilever. A cantilever is a beam which is fixed at one end but free at the other, like a diving board.

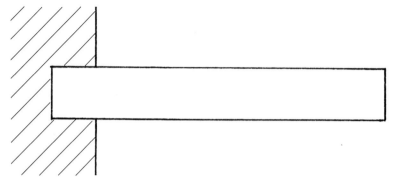

Fig. 17: A cantilevered beam

Clearly a bridge with a gap at one end would be less than satisfactory. But a bridge that has to open does well to be free at one end so that its platform can be rotated upwards. A draw bridge is a hinged platform that is held up at its free end by ropes, cables or chains, i.e. flexible tension members, when being raised and functions as a cantilever, but when lowered and in place, becomes a simply-supported beam hinged at one end and supported from below at the other. The simplest form of cantilever bridge is made from two beams, each fixed at opposite sides of the gap and extending to meet the other in the middle. When they join they become a beam clamped at each end. It is therefore only a cantilever during construction. Although the construction process increases the stress on each beam, requiring the beam to be made more robustly, it avoids the need for expensive centring. Another variant is to build cantilevered beams out from both sides of a pier simultaneously, forming a balanced cantilever, and then joining them directly, or with a central suspended section, to the similarly-constructed beam approaching from the other bank. The beams can be made from steel trusses or pre-stressed concrete. Large bridges often need to support the cantilevered arms with tension members above the carriageway and compression members below. This means that large towers have to be built above the piers to provide anchor points for the tension members.

A cantilever bridge made from steel can be made to massive proportions

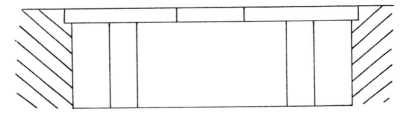

Fig. 18: A cantilever bridge

such as in the Forth Bridge. This has three large and complicated steel tow-ers, each with four pillars, to support the carriageway and to provide anchor points for the tension and compression members reaching symmetrically outwards on each side. There are suspended trusses over the two main sea-ways and steel trusses supported on masonry piers at each end of the bridge. This has provided a strong and rigid structure which bridged an enormous gap and allowed considerable headroom for ships to pass underneath, albeit at the cost of massive amounts of steel (and paint!). The original plan to cross this formidable obstacle was a suspension bridge designed by Sir Thomas Bouch but the failure of his Tay Bridge led to a loss of confidence and work was stopped after the foundation stone was laid.

The Forth Bridge was built as balanced cantilevers from each tower using creeper cranes. All bridges are vulnerable before they are complete. This was spectacularly demonstrated by the collapse of the central span of the Quebec Bridge, a similar bridge to the Forth, in 1907 which killed 74 of the men working on it. The cause of this disaster was that the steel can-tilever tower on the south side proved too weak to support the weight of the central suspended span as it was being built out from it. In turn this was caused by poor organisation and a failure to recalculate the loads and stresses when the original span had been increased by 61 metres.

This particular crossing seems to have been cursed. When the replace-ment, and much heavier, bridge was being built in 1917 it was decided to build the central span in one piece and lift it into place using hydraulic jacks. During this manoeuvre the span slipped out of its stirrups and crashed into the river killing eleven men. Both Quebec bridges were of cantilever design but similar mishaps can occur with other types.

Generally compression structures are easier and safer to build than ten-sion structures. Nevertheless some of the earliest bridges were tension structures. Primitive suspension bridges were, and still are, built using ropes made from creepers or bamboo swung, thrown or floated across rivers in deep gorges. Some have a single rope and people crossing them hold onto a loop around the rope and descend, presumably fairly rapidly, to the lowest point and then have to haul themselves, or be hauled, up to the far side. More sophisticated versions have baskets. In ancient China travellers carried with them a wooden saddle with a deep groove in the underside to accommodate the rope. More elaborate bridges had an additional rope to act as a 'hand rail' and some had cross ropes to make floors and sides. In the 1930s a group of pygmies in the Congo was filmed making a rope bridge. The first rope was suspended from a tall tree and a small boy hanging onto the end of the rope was encouraged to swing with ever increasing amplitude until he managed to grab a branch on the far side of the river. Once the rope was secured, the boy clambered back and the first rope was used to carry others across the river. After six days a 50 metre-long, half-tubular bridge had been constructed (Brown).

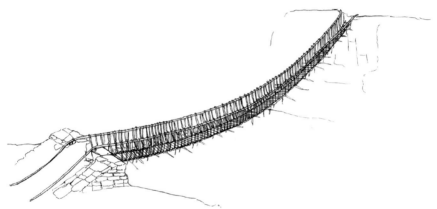

Fig. 19: A rope bridge

These bridges are easy and quick to construct although they make crossing an unnerving process because of their lack of rigidity. Their strength depends on the tensile strength of the ropes used to make them and how well, and to what, they are attached on each bank. The materials from which they are made deteriorate quite rapidly with time and moisture and some are only intended to last a single season. They are constructed from several strands of creeper or lengths of rope so there is little risk of them all failing at the same instant unless the load is massively excessive, but they are vulnerable to progressive failure when increasing stress is placed on the remaining strands. They have obvious limitations as far as animals and vehicles are concerned. In spite of this, primitive suspension bridges continue to play an important role in many parts ot the world, indeed temporary military bridges are sometimes still built in this way. They have also evolved into one of the most successful of all bridges – the modern suspension bridge.

The modern suspension bridge is perhaps the most elegant of the big bridges. It is amazingly delicate considering the size of span often achieved. Although still largely tension structures their design has some important differences from the primitive version described above. The features of a modern suspension bridge were first defined by an American called James Finley who went on to build several small bridges based on them. In the first place the walkway or roadway is largely level across its span, i.e. it does not sag. Also it is flat across its width and is generally some form of truss and is not the main load-bearing structure. The weight of the bridge is carried in separate cables passing over high and relatively massive towers at each end and firmly anchored into rock or large concrete blocks some distance on the land side of the towers. The roadway is suspended from these bridging cables by thinner, generally vertical, cables and usually forms a shallow arch in the process. The bridging and suspending cables are all in tension and the supporting towers are heavily in compression. Although the roadway may be an arch it is too weak to be self-supporting and usually does not have load-bearing abutments at each end; it acts as a series of beams carrying the loads between the suspending cables. It also needs to be stiff enough to resist the unwanted movements that suspension bridges are prone to and which will be discussed later. Nowadays the roadways are made of steel and the towers from steel or concrete but in earlier versions the towers were of masonry and some had

Plate 36: The suspension bridge over the River Lowther.

wrought-iron chains instead of cables and roadways made of wooden planks.

The first substantial modern suspension bridge, the Union Bridge across the River Tweed between England and Scotland, was built by Samuel Brown in 1820. In the Lake District there is a small suspension bridge with wooden towers over the River Lowther under Knipe Scar (NY515193). (To view it go through Bampton to Bampton Grange and turn left onto the minor road towards Knipe Moor. Where the road branches to Askham, take the footpath that heads diagonally downhill towards the river for about 350 metres. The bridge is marked on the OS map.)

The modern suspension bridge is built by constructing the towers first and then by suspending a set of light cables from anchorage to anchorage to support a 'traveller' that has wheels running on top of the cables. Winches pull the traveller from one end of the bridge to the other while it carries a loop of wire to form a strand of the main suspensory cable. When several of these have been bundled together to complete the main cables, the suspending cables are attached to them at intervals by 'clamping bands.' Prefabricated sections of roadway are then lifted into place and attached to the bottom of the suspending cables.

Alternatively the roadway is cantilevered out from each tower, being attached to the overhead cables as it progresses. With this approach the roadway initially slopes downwards as it extends from the tower. This is because the weight of the roadway extending out from the tower, say at about a quarter of the span, distorts the shape of the overhead cable so that it sags just above the roadway but moves upwards at the centre of the span where the roadway is yet to be attached. (The cable is a constant length, so if part of the curve is pulled down another part must rise up.) As the roadway extends towards the centre of the span, its weight pulls the central length of the cable downwards, raising the parts of the roadway near to the towers so that it assumes its final shape. The initial curve of the, unloaded, suspensory cables is a catenary which gradually changes towards a parabola as the roadway is fully attached (see chapter 7), although in

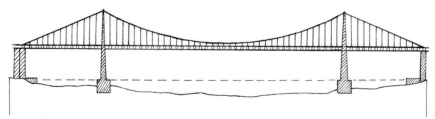

Fig. 20: A modern suspension bridge

practice the shape is not very different. Interestingly the taller the towers the smaller the stress on the main cables which can then be made thinner but of course also need to be longer.

Clearly a suspension bridge would fail if the bridging cables snapped or parted from their anchorages, although being made of multiple parts this would be unlikely to happen all at once but there is always the risk of progressive failure. A recently-discovered problem is corrosion of the cables, which has caused some wires to snap, even though they are contained within a weatherproof sleeve. The older bridges were more vulnerable as they had many fewer wrought iron chains than wires in a suspensory cable. Also, in theory, the towers could collapse under excessive compression but this is unlikely. In fact it is the very elegance and lightness of these bridges that has proved to be their occasional undoing.

The roadway of a suspension bridge is not rigid and can move in three dimensions. An up and down movement, rather like a wave, can be produced by a vehicle moving along the roadway (the live load) or just by the action of the wind (an environmental load). A sideways swing can be caused by the live load moving from side to side or from wind forces and there can also be a rotating movement produced by the wind. Historically, and not so historically, all three have produced problems and even complete failures.

Any non-rigid structure has a tendency to move rhythmically, or resonate, at a particular frequency, called its natural frequency. Any mechanism that reinforces these movements rapidly increases their size. This is what happens when you give little pushes to a child on a swing. As long as each push is synchronised with the swing's existing movements the amplitude builds up rapidly and pretty soon the swing is almost horizontal and the child's enthusiasm tends to evaporate. Desynchronising the pushes rapidly stops it. As you might expect, suspension bridges, being non-rigid, are prey to resonance from any regular pulsations of load, even the regular pacing of pedestrians. This is the reason for marching soldiers breaking step when going over a suspension bridge. This was known to the Roman army but apparently not to the British and French armies. In 1831 Broughton suspension bridge in Manchester collapsed when soldiers were marching over it and, more disastrously, in 1850 the suspension bridge at Angers, in France, was destroyed by 478 soldiers marching over it in step, killing 226 of them, although overload may also have been a factor here.

A variation of this vertical resonance is horizontal resonance, made famous by the Millennium Bridge over the Thames when it was first opened in 2000, although it had been seen before. This was caused by the small lateral forces generated by people as they walked over the bridge producing lateral oscillations in the bridge which in turn made the pedestrians sway more and in synchrony and so on until the whole bridge 'wobbled'. Experiments carried out after the bridge had been closed to the public showed that the movements did not build up gradually but suddenly developed after a critical number of pedestrians (around 170) walked over one span. Stiffening the bridge was impractical and the problem was managed by attaching passive dampers to the structure. A damper is a mechanism for reducing the amplitude of oscillations by converting their energy into other forms, such as heat, in this case by using 37 pistons in fluid-filled cylinders. As a precaution 52 tuned mass dampers (essentially weights on springs) were attached under the deck to reduce any vertical oscillations.

A suspension bridge over the River Tees built in the early nineteenth century was used in an experiment to carry trains on the Stockton and Darlington Railway although it had originally been intended for road vehicles. It was reported that, "The platform rose up three feet before the locomotive at ordinary speed; and that the entire work was nearly destroyed by the passage of the train." In 1830 another suspension bridge, over the River Esk at Montrose, suffered a snapped chain as 700 people watching a boat race rushed from one side to the other, many falling into the river and drowning. But the best known, and most spectacular, failure was that of the Tacoma Narrows Bridge near Seattle, not least because its death throes were recorded on film (see the Tacoma Narrows Bridge websites). The mechanism of its failing was an excessive twist.

The Tacoma Narrows Bridge developed a reputation for undue movement even while it was being built and the construction workers on its roadway were often sick with its excessive vibration. When it was opened to traffic it attracted people keen to experience its movements and crossing it was considered as exciting as, and not dissimilar to, a short sea crossing. The bridge, christened 'Galloping Gertie', would sway from side to side in even mild wind but the main movement was a wave with one half of the length of the bridge going up while the other moved down. It was so marked that vehicles coming in the opposite direction often became invisible behind the wave.

These movements were caused by "periodic vortex shedding" forming a "Karman vortex street." This is a phenomenon that can affect most long, slim structures such as bridges and chimneys exposed to wind. Indeed many modern, and relatively flimsy, sheet metal chimneys have spiral 'strakes' to prevent damage from it. As air (or any fluid) moves past such a structure, a vortex (fluid moving in a spiral, for example going down a plug hole) grows from part of the structure until it reaches a size at which it is torn away by the flow. Another vortex then starts to form and for a constant wind speed the process repeats regularly. As the vortices are shed, asymmetric flow patterns develop, producing areas of pressure difference, which give regular pushes to the structure. For a bridge with a wide horizontal roadway, the crucial force is vertically up and down.

The frequency of this cycle of vortex formation increases as the wind speed increases, so on occasion the wind will 'find' a resonance. This produced the standing waves that made the approaching cars invisible to each other. In this case the roadway behaves rather like a piano wire which has been made to vibrate. The vibration with the longest wavelength (the fundamental) involves the whole wire moving up and down synchronously, with the largest amplitude in the centre and stationary points at each end. With a suspension bridge this is unlikely to happen because the suspensory cables do not stretch much and therefore inhibit the downward movement of the whole length of the roadway in one big wave. Shorter wavelengths, however, are possible and the number of stationary points, or nodes, along the Tacoma bridge increased with the ambient wind speed.

But it was an unusual rotational movement that proved to be its (literal) downfall. As winds passing at right angles to a bridge are usually not exactly horizontal they tend to push one side of the roadway up or down. The side of the roadway away from the wind will then twist in the opposite direction. If the roadway is not sufficiently stiff or wide these twisting movements can become larger and larger. It can be seen that if this situation gets out of control the bridge, or at least the roadway, will twist itself to destruction as it snaps its suspending cables and develops progressive failure; which is exactly what happened to the Tacoma Narrows Bridge on 7 November 1940. Amazingly the only fatality was a three-legged dog called Tubby that was left in a car marooned on the bridge and bit his would-be rescuer. The bridge had been open for just over four months.

The technical explanation for the cause of these events has been disputed over the years but the current view is that it owed more to aeroelastic flutter than the periodic vortex shedding described above or resonance triggered by wind turbulence. Flutter is a vibration produced by aerodynamic forces – in this case the wind – acting on an object – in this case the roadway of the bridge – so as to produce increasing and potentially destructive movements. These increasing movements occur when a positive feedback loop develops between the aerodynamic forces and the structure's natural vibration. Flutter became well know in aeronautical circles as a cause of wings snapping off when aircraft stopped being biplanes (i.e. when their wings were braced together to form a stiff truss system) and became monoplanes.

As above, wind coming from the side and below the roadway will lift that edge of the platform, particularly when it is already lifted by the lon-gitudinal waves also mentioned above. The actual mechanism of lift seems to have been produced by the formation and drifting of large-scale vortices above and below the platform. This is different from the periodic vortex shedding mentioned previously which had a different frequency for this structure. As one side of the platform lifts the opposite side rotates downwards. The roadway has torsional stiffness and strain energy builds up with the degree of rotation and eventually this, together with the plat-form stalling, overcomes the wind-induced lift and the rotation reverses and tends to overshoot. If the overshoot is big enough, the wind then push-es the upper side of the roadway downwards increasing the amplitude of the overshoot. This, in its turn, is reversed by the strain-energy build up in the roadway and the rotation reverses again. It can be seen that this process produces rotational vibrations which in the case of the Tacoma bridge went on to cause structural failure. For the same reason that the fundamental longitudinal wave is prevented by the main cables not stretching, the fundamental twisting wave is inhibited and a torsional node developed halfway along the bridge. Not surprisingly this was the point of failure as the roadway twisted in opposite directions here.

This was not the first time that a suspension bridge had shown destructive twisting movements. During a storm in 1854 the suspension bridge over the Ohio River at Wheeling in the United States, at that time the longest span in the world, developed longitudinal waves and then twisting waves with a node at the centre of the span. Most of the bridge collapsed but in due course it was repaired and stiffened and has survived to become a national monument.

Ironically the original plan for the Tacoma Narrows Bridge, produced by the Washington State Engineer, had been of conventional design, with 7.6 metre girders below the roadway to stiffen it. Its cost had been estimated at $11 million but the commissioning authority had been swayed by the $8 million estimate produced by a New York group led by Leon Moisseiff, the then doyen of American bridge design. His bridge used girders only 2.4 metres deep. The Tacoma bridge ended up with an unfortunate combination of a long span, narrow roadway, little torsional stiffness, a bluff or un-streamlined deck and a windy location. The solution was to go back to using a stiffening truss under the roadway, such as in the Forth Road Bridge, or, more economically, to have a shape that has low aerodynamic resistance (an aerofoil) as well as being even more stiff because it is a closed box girder, such as the Severn and Humber Bridges. Damping also helps. The replacement for the Tacoma Narrows Bridge was actually longer but had a substantial truss below the deck, stiffening struts and openings in the roadway to let wind through. In contrast to its predecessor it became known as 'Sturdy Girtie'. It has since been joined by a second bridge.

Although we have dealt at some length with the vulnerabilities of suspension bridges, perhaps because bridges that fall down are more interesting than bridges that stay up, they are still the best choice, often the only choice, for crossing really large gaps.

Suspension bridges are generally not stable enough for trains to use, although there have been one or two, such as the Niagara Falls Suspension Bridge in 1855.*   Trains need flat rigid and strong bridges. In the early railways this was provided by masonry arches below the track but in more recent times steel has been used. For small spans this was often in the form of simply supported beams or girders.

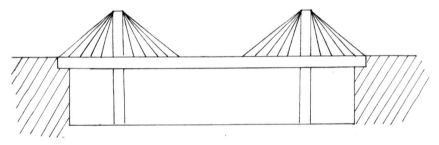

Fig. 21: A cable-stayed bridge

A bridge that has much of the elegance of a suspension bridge is the cable-stayed bridge. Like the suspension bridge it has high towers, or sometimes a single tower, with cables running down to support the roadway on each side of the towers. Unlike the suspension bridge, however, the cables run directly to the roadway and do not form a continuous curve for separate, vertical tension members to carry the roadway. This means that the cables pull towards the tower and not straight up as in a suspension bridge. The roadway therefore has to be more substantial to resist this compressive force, which makes the bridge more rigid. On the other hand, the land-side cable anchorages do not need to be as strong because the towers are more balanced by having cables running on each side. Land

---

* The builder who started the project, Charles Ellet, used a kite to carry first line across the gap and then built a suspension footbridge. He left after a dispute and the main bridge was built by John Augustus Roebling of Brooklyn Bridge fame, who used the footbridge as scaffolding. It was initially made of wood but was gradually replaced by steel. It was dismantled in 1897. Mark Twain found crossing it something of a trial because of the vibration caused by the trains.

anchorages may even be superfluous if the bridge has equal spans on each side of the towers.

The bridge is in effect a cantilever with the cable tension members holding it up and is built in the same manner as a balanced-cantilever bridge, edging out on each side of the towers at roughly equal rates. The cables are said to be either of a fan design, where they all come from the top of the towers, or a harp where the shorter parallel cables come from further down. The harp design produces a bending force on the tower whereas the more efficient fan produces mainly axial compression. An early example was the Dryburgh Abbey Bridge over the River Tweed. It was built in 1817 but lasted less than six months before collapsing. The cable-stayed bridge is most economic for spans between those of cantilever and suspension bridges.

Most bridges are over water and as water is used for shipping there may be a conflict of passage unless the bridge is high enough to allow ships beneath it. One recent solution to this problem is the Oresund Bridge between Sweden and Denmark which is part bridge and part tunnel, the two being joined by an artificial island. A more common approach is to build a bridge that allows normal road passage most of the time but gets out of the way of shipping when it has to. One method of doing this is to have a central pier with a truss or tied-arch rotating on it, such as the Armstrong Swing Bridge in Newcastle upon Tyne. This is an economical way of supporting the massive weight of a steel girder bridge but divides the river into two equal channels and presents all the problems of building piers. An alternative is to have a bridge that lifts out of the way. This may be a simple drawbridge using ropes, cables or chains to lift a hinged platform but larger versions need a balancing counterweight (a bascule bridge), such as Tower Bridge in London, to make the work of lifting easier. Other variations are the lift bridge where the whole bridge platform is

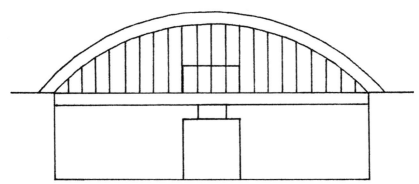

Fig. 22: A swing bridge.

lifted vertically by mechanisms in towers at each end, the table bridge where a similar section is pushed up from below or even submerged deeply enough to allow ships to pass over it.

A newer development is the tilting bridge, such as the Gateshead Millennium Bridge, which has two parabolic arches of the same span able to rotate about a common horizontal axis. When the bridge is closed to navigation the walkway is almost horizontal with its arch pointing down river. It is suspended by cables from a more vertical arch which leans away from it. To open the bridge the arches are rotated synchronously in the up river direction by hydralic rams. The upper arch therefore becomes more horizontal as the lower arch becomes more vertical, rather in the manner of raising a visor, thereby increasing the clearance below the walkway. A transporter bridge, such as the one in Middlesborough, moves a short road section from one side of the river to the other by suspending it by cables from a high overhead structure, so allowing massive headroom for shipping. It is 'a bridge that thinks it's a ferry' and, like a ferry, severely limits the crossing traffic. It is probably an evolutionary blind alley in bridge design and nowadays it is more of an engineering curiosity.

Yet another type of bridge is the floating bridge where the road platform rests on a series of floats, or pontoons, tied together and stretching across the river. As the pontoons will tend to be pushed down river each end of the platform has to be securely tethered to the bank. They are useful for long crossings in sheltered waters but have been mainly employed as temporary military bridges. They have a long history, probably starting in the ninth century BC in China, and were also used by the ancient

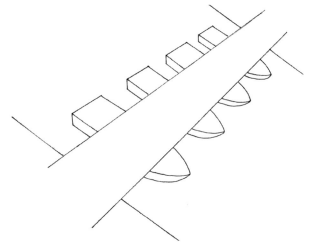

Fig. 23: A pontoon bridge

Persians, Greeks and Romans. An impressive example was built in 480BC by Xerxes, son of the more-famous Darius. It was to cross the Hellespont, now better known as the Dardanelles, a distance of more than one and a half kilometres. It was said to consist of two rows of boats, 360 on the Black Sea side and 314 on the other, connected by flax and papyrus ropes and the roadway planked, then covered with soil and protected by a paling on each side. This was his second attempt, the first bridge having been destroyed by a storm. It is said that Xerxes responded to this by having the builders beheaded and the waters of the straits lashed. No doubt the commissioners of more modern, failed, bridges have had similar feelings.

The weight-carrying ability of a pontoon bridge depends on the mass of water displaced by individual pontoons. They are even more unstable than suspension bridges and can oscillate in all three dimensions. Once again soldiers should brake step when crossing. Another disadvantage is that they usually block the river to shipping although a movable section can be provided. They are also vulnerable to objects floating down the river, such as mines in a war zone, and like all boats, pontoons can spring leaks and sink.

Another military 'bridge' was the underwater bridge used by the German army in World War II. This was essentially a reinforced ford that allowed heavy vehicles to cross but would remain invisible from the air and hence difficult to destroy, although the approach roads could still be a give-away.

This has been a brief catalogue of some of the different designs of bridge. Not all of them can be found in the Lake District but if you had to travel there perhaps you might have seen other types on the way.

7: MORE ABOUT STONE ARCHES

Stone arches were introduced in chapter one but armed with the material from the previous chapter we can look at them again, this time in more detail.

The concept of the 'line of thrust' can be extended to arches. In this case the line runs roughly through the middle of the individual stones and sideways out into the abutments as well as downwards into the ground.

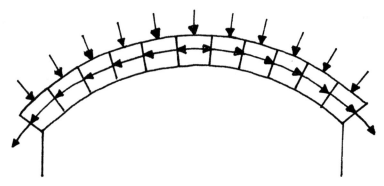

Fig. 24: The line of thrust in a stone arch

The forces on the abutments of an arched bridge can be divided into those directed vertically downwards and those horizontally outwards. Just considering the dead load of the bridge and assuming that the abutments are both at the same level, the vertical thrust downwards is the weight of the bridge divided equally between the two abutments, just like a beam:-

$$V = \frac{M L g}{2}$$

where V = vertical thrust downwards
M = mass per unit length of bridge
L = length of bridge
g = acceleration due to gravity

The horizontal, outwards thrust depends on the flatness of the arch and even more on its length:-

$$H = \frac{M L^2 g}{8 d}$$

where H = horizontal thrust outwards
d = the rise of the arch.

So flattish arches with long spans need strong abutments which are very resistant to lateral thrust.

The most efficient shape for an arch that is just supporting its own weight is an inverted catenary. A catenary, from the Latin for a chain, is the shape taken up by a uniform and infinitely flexible chain or rope with its ends fixed and acted upon only by the force of gravity. This was first realised by our old friend Robert Hooke in 1670 and published by him in 1675 as another of his latin anagrams, "As hangs a flexible cable, so inverted, stand the touching pieces of an arch." Hooke's executor eventually published the solution in 1705 although it had been deciphered before then. The mathematics of the catenary eluded Hooke however and had to wait until 1691 for Leibniz, Huygens and Johann Bernoulli to publish the equation.*

A flexible cable, hanging under its own weight, will follow the forces acting on it in the most efficient and economical fashion. Consider the cable as a lot of small segments joined end to end. At the top, next to one of the fixed ends, the main force acting on the first segment is the weight of all the segments below it pulling it down together with a smaller force pulling it across to the other fixed point. As a result it becomes almost vertical. Moving down the cable there are fewer and fewer segments below so the downwards pull is less and the segments become more and more horizontal and ultimately completely horizontal at the lowest point. In other words the downwards forces acting on the cable are not uniform and decrease towards the midpoint while the horizontal force stays the same.

As Hooke said, an arch can be considered to be an inverted cable, if you like thickened and frozen so it stays rigid. As the shape of the hanging cable is the most efficient it follows that the shape of the inverted-catenary arch is also the most efficient. The inverted-catenary arch was much used by the Catalan architect Antoni Gaudi. The attic ceiling of the Casa Mila, for example, in Barcelona, is constructed from innumerable inverted-catenary arches and makes an unusual and wonderful sight. But few arches are built just as arches, they are generally built to support something else, such as a

---

* Johann was not the famous Bernoulli – Daniel – who gave us his Principle and helped us to fly, but his father. The catenary problem was posed by Johann's brother, Jakob. This was a remarkable mathematical family, there were also Nicolaus I and II. As in many families, talented or otherwise, there was a family feud. Johann became jealous of his son's success, tried to steal some of his work and ultimately banished Daniel from the family home.

roadway or a building. Even Gaudi altered the shapes of his load-bearing
catenary arches by making scale models from threads with little bags
hanging from them weighted to represent the forces acting at these points.
An exception is the free-standing 'Gateway Arch' in Saint Louis,
Missouri, which even has its equation inscribed inside the arch.

A catenary is the shape of a cable under gravity if its weight per unit
length of cable is uniform. A parabola (a section of a cone whose plane is
parallel to a side other than the base) is the shape of a cable under gravity
if its weight is uniform per unit horizontal length. The most efficient shape
for a horizontally-and-uniformly-loaded arch is therefore a parabola. This
is a similar shape to a catenary, which is a hyperbola, another conic section, and the two are often confused, indeed Hooke may have done so, but
the two are distinct and cannot be transposed.

The change in the shape of the curve of the main cable of a suspension
bridge during its construction is a demonstration of a catenary becoming a
parabola. Building a modern suspension bridge starts with the two towers.
When they have reached their full heights the main suspensory cables are
spun from one anchorage, over the towers to the other anchorage and then
back and forth until the full cable is completed. As the cables hang by
themselves the forces acting on them are from the weight of the cable
alone and they assume the shape of a catenary. The roadway is then constructed below the main cables and hung from them by the suspending
cables. The roadway is of uniform weight and is far heavier than the main
cables. It therefore imposes far greater forces acting vertically downwards
at intervals on these cables. As the roadway is of uniform weight these
forces are also pretty well uniform along its length and the shape of the
curve of the main cables changes to reflect this and becomes (close to) a
parabola.

Like the frozen catenary we imagined before, an arched bridge can be
considered to be an inverted suspension bridge, so the most efficient shape
for an arch carrying a uniform load along its length is a parabola.

Gaudi's catenary arches were tall and thin but bridges need to be wide
and flat i.e. to have a large span for a low rise. It is therefore just the part
of the curve near to the vertex that is relevant for bridge design and here
there is little difference between a catenary and a parabola. Also the load
on a bridge changes as things move along it so the total load is not uniform
and the line of thrust through it will change position. As long as the thickness of the arch is great enough the line of thrust will stay within its middle third and all will be well. If it moves outside the middle third the stresses on the material that makes up the arch will increase and, depending on
its strength, cracks may appear. If the line of thrust moves to the inside of

the arch this part will be in greater compression but the outer circumference at this point will be in tension and any crack will develop here. Tall, pointed arches are prone to crack at the outer surface of the apex because the line of thrust forms a curve rather than a point. It is doubtful that the builders of the Lake District stone arches were much taxed by the subtleties of catenaries and parabolas but builders of thin, elegant arches need to be more careful that they get their sums right.

Much of the evolution of the design of masonry bridges over the years has consisted of flattening arches and increasing spans, successive generations drawing courage and confidence from earlier successes. Having said that, it took a long time for Western bridge builders to reach the sophistication of the An Ji Bridge at Zhao Xian in China which was built in the seventh century and had an extremely shallow and delicate segmental arch with two open arches in each spandrel wall.

Another variation occurs where the two ends of the bridge are not directly opposite each other. This produces a skew bridge, or even a skew viaduct, with complicated stone or brick work such as the one at Burnstones, north of Alston (NY675544). This is an interesting bridge for another reason – it has six arches on one side and five on the other.

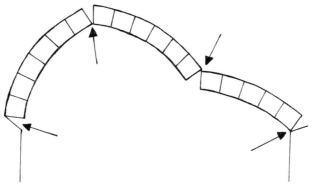

Fig. 25: A stone arched bridge with four hinge points and therefore failing

Once built, arches are very forgiving structures. Unlike a beam, the point at which an arch is most likely to fail is not at the centre but somewhere between one quarter to rather less than half way along its span. In fact an arch needs a minimum of four breaks, or hinge points, to fail completely. If an arch does fail, one part falls in, usually at the point of the load, and another is simultaneously pushed out and this may happen explosively with little warning. Even if part of an arch is destroyed, so long as not too great a length disappears, the rest of the arch may just join up to make a flatter arch. High Sweden Bridge near Ambleside has a flattened arch but seems perfectly safe. This inherent stability explains why arched bridges are difficult to blow up behind retreating armies and why so many have survived from antiquity. Gordon adds that to blow up an arched bridge you have to dig down in four places, preferably at each end and at the junctions of each third, to reach the arch itself and this may well take time as it will probably be covered with fill and surfaced with something hard. If the enemy is close behind it is easy to see why this may be an unattractive proposition. Destroying beam bridges is a much easier proposition. Another reason for the survival of arches may be that the wedge-shaped stones are less useful to the local peasantry bent on recycling old buildings.

Some arches are built with hinges to allow for movement imposed by loads, thermal expansion or settlement of the abutments. The Tyne Bridge in Newcastle has two massive hinges between the arch and the bases of the abutments to allow for some rotation. Simple arch bridges, such as the ones in the Lake District, do not have built-in hinges and are said to be 'statically indeterminate'. This means that it is not possible (easily) to calculate the forces in the structure from a knowledge of the loads acting on it. There are historical 'rules of thumb' and mathematical approximations of varying complexity but these will not be considered here. An arch with two hinge points is still statically indeterminate but one with three, such as Monkwearmouth Bridge in Sunderland and many concrete motorway foot bridges, can be relatively easily analysed. They are also good at dealing with expansion and settlement although in other respects they are less efficient structurally.

Superficially similar to a railway viaduct is the masonry aqueduct. An aqueduct is a waterproof trough which gently slopes to allow water to flow under gravity. This means that they have to be carried across valleys and gorges without losing much in the way of height. Ancient Rome had eleven such aqueducts with a total length of about 560 kilometres of which some 60 kilometres was carried above ground on multiple arches. Arguably the most impressive Roman aqueduct to have survived is the three-tiered Pont du Gard near Avignon in France built about 19BC. Interestingly the arches in the lower two tiers are not the usual Roman 3:1 arch to pier ratio but more like 5:1 although the top tier is almost 1:1.

Even canals have been built as aqueducts to avoid using tedious series of locks or to cross rivers. The first in England was the Barton Aqueduct built by James Brindley in 1761 to carry the Bridgewater Canal over the River Irwell near Manchester. It was replaced by an even more remarkable swing aqueduct built in 1893 by Edward Williams over what had now become the Manchester Ship Canal. Persons worried about the effect that a string of loaded barges might have on the structure of the aqueduct should ponder the consequences of Archimedes Principle. There is an open aqueduct on the hill side above the north west part of Thirlmere which is crossed by the route over Sticks Pass but unfortunately it is firmly attached to the ground. The Thirlmere to Manchester aqueduct breaks cover in several places to cross ravines or streams, such as crossing Tongue Gill, north of Grasmere (NY338095), near Michael's Fold, again north of Grasmere (NY344084) and Dunny Beck near Whitemoss Common, between Grasmere and Rydal (NY349070). All of these are covered aqueducts. (If you wish to view them the one crossing Tongue Gill is at the bottom of a steep-sided ravine. Access is difficult and dangerous and is not advised.

The other two are much easier. For Michael's Fold take the minor road that leaves the A591 next to The Swan Hotel in Grasmere. Turn left where the road forks and shortly afterwards turn right up a narrow tarmac road heading uphill. It has a sign post to Alcock Tarn. At the top of this road go through a gate and take the middle of the three paths, to go straight ahead. The aqueduct is about five minutes walk along this path. It has two arches, slightly separated, each over a different stream.

For Dunney Beck start on the wide path at the Rydal end of the car park on the north side of White Moss Common, between Grasmere and Rydal. Follow this path uphill as it curves to the left and ultimately joins the coffin route from Rydal to Grasmere. Turn right onto this road and after about 200 metres turn left through a gate with a National Trust sign and head up hill on a narrow path with Dunney Beck on your right. The aqueduct is about 100 metres along this path.

Long masonry bridges have to be built with multiple arches which introduces the problems of building piers down to the river bed. To build them in anything other than shallow and slow-moving rivers temporary enclosures, called coffer dams, have to be used to keep the water out and piles may need to be driven down to reach bed rock capable of supporting the arch and pier. Deep water requires the use of a caisson. This is a metal

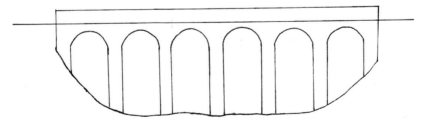

Fig. 26: A multi-arch masonry bridge

cylinder that sits on the river bed, its bottom end open to allow work to be carried out on the river bed while water is kept out by pressurising the cylinder with compressed air. This adds the chance of developing the bends, or caisson's disease, to the risks of drowning.*

Not only is a pier difficult and dangerous to construct it can fail later on if the river bed is damaged. As the water flows past a pier it dives and produces a vortex. These vortices then move along both sides of the pier removing river bed as they go, a process called scour. All this can lead to the river bed being excavated around the up-stream end of the pier with the risk of it collapsing into the river. Streamlining at the up-stream end of the pier greatly reduces vortex formation and hence scour and at the down-stream end it reduces the size of the wake region. In addition piers obstruct the flow of the river, particularly if they collect rubbish, and increase the velocity of the flow, producing even more scour. The old London Bridge had eighteen piers resting on large, boat-shaped cutwaters producing fierce currents in the channels between them. This led to considerable scour and an almost continuous need for repair. For most of the time London Bridge really was 'falling down'. If possible, piers are better avoided but even bridges without piers can be damaged by scour, particularly if built on a bend or if the river changes course and undermines the abutments. Some bridges even have a masonry pavement built on the river bed beneath them to prevent scour, such as the one at Coldstream built by John Smeaton of Eddystone Lighthouse fame (NT849401).

This completes the brief survey of bridge types with details of their design and construction. The building of masonry bridges is largely a thing of the past. Nowadays there are quicker and cheaper solutions that have greater appeal for the bodies that finance their construction. Nevertheless we are fortunate in the United Kingdom to have inherited a fine collection of old stone bridges of which the Lake District packhorse bridges form a small, but in my view delightful, part.

---

* At least one famous bridge builder, Washington Roebling, became paralysed as a result of developing the bends. He was one of the builders of the Brooklyn Bridge in New York. He had taken over from his father who planned the bridge but had died as a consequence of an accident during the early building works. Washington's wife, Emily, taught herself enough maths and engineering to complete the bridge.

A FEW WORDS ABOUT FELL WALKING

Many of the walks in this book are serious treks across the high fells of the Lake District. This is an area well known for its heavy rainfall, strong winds and cloud bases which stretch below the mountain tops, particularly at times outside the summer months. For these reasons it is important to follow some simple precautions.

1) Be aware of the weather forecast for your particular area and plan your walk accordingly. A low cloud base makes navigation much more difficult. Snow makes walking much slower, more tiring and more dangerous. Ice can be even more hazardous and is common on the stone paths in winter. Even rain can cause significant chilling, particularly in association with wind. What may be a pleasant winter's day on the valley floor can be an Arctic environment on the summits.

2) Be able to navigate. You must have an appropriate map (such as the OS 1:25,000) of the area you intend to visit and the areas that you might stray into. This may mean carrying two or three maps. You should be able to use a compass, even in poor weather conditions and under the stress of feeling lost. You should also be able to 'read' the map, in other words be able to relate its symbols and lines to the topography. If necessary, go on a navigation course. Most of the navigation in the Lake District is just knowing where you are on a path but even this can be difficult in mist when the path disappears temporarily and the distant markers have vanished. A GPS (global positioning system) device, and knowing how to use it, can be very useful in these circumstances.

3) Know your intended route and tell someone where you are going and when you expect to return.

4) It is safer to walk as part of a group, even if it is just two people.

5) Take an adequate supply of food and drinking fluid. Hot weather increases the consumption of fluid considerably.

6) Wear appropriate clothing and footwear and carry extra warm clothing (including gloves and a hat) in case the temperature drops. There is always a temperature drop with increasing altitude and it is often combined with an increasing wind speed.

7) The walks in this book are almost entirely along public paths however one or two of the bridges are on private land. If you want to visit them it is only polite to ask the permission of the land owner first. I have always found them to be rather proud of their bridges and happy to allow you to view them. Several even took the trouble to show me exactly where they were and to tell me what they knew about them. I can understand that this might change should the flow of bridge voyeurs become too great so some tact and the occasional tactical withdrawal might be needed here.

BIBLIOGRAPHY

Bowtell H D, *Rails through Lakeland*, Silver Link Publishing, St. Michael's on Wye, 1989.

Brown D J, *Bridges: Three thousand years of defying nature,* Mitchell Beazley, London, 1993.

Colingwood W G, *Packhorse-bridges*, Transactions of the Cumberland and Westmorland Antiquarian and Archaeological Society, 28, p120-128, 1928.

Gies J, *Bridges and men*, Doubleday, New York, 1963

Gordon J E, *Structures*, Penguin, Harmondsworth, 1978.

Gordon J E, *The new science of strong materials*, Penguin, Harmondsworth, 1968.

Hinchliffe E, *A guide to the packhorse bridges of England*, Cicerone, Milnthorpe, 1994.

Hindle P, *Roads and tracks of the Lake District*, Cicerone, Milnthorpe, 1998.

Hopkins H J, *A span of bridges*, David and Charles, Newton Abbot, 1970.

Langmuir E, *Mountaincraft and leadership*, Third Edition (revised), The Scottish Sports Council, Edinburgh and The Mountain Leader Training Board, Manchester, 1995.

Larsen A, *Aerodynamics of the Tacoma Narrows Bridge - 60 years later,* Structural Engineering International, 10, 4, 243-248, 2000.

Levy M, Salvadori M, *Why buildings fall down,* W W Norton & Co., New York, 1992.

Linklater M, *Big stone man bridged our burn*, The Times, London, 12 July 2003.

Orrell R, *Saddle tramp in the Lake District*, Robert Hale, London, 1979.

Page J (editor), *Masonry arch bridges*, HMSO, London, 1993.

Readyhough G, *The Lake District: The ultimate guide*, Hayloft, Kirkby Stephen, 2004.

Salvadori M, *Why buildings stand up. The strength of architecture*, W W Norton & Co., New York, 1980.

Wainwright A, *A pictorial guide to the lakeland fells*, Seven volumes, Westmorland Gazette, Kendal, 1955 to 1966.

Wainwright A, *Fellwalking with Wainwright*, Michael Joseph, London, 1984.

Wainwright A, *Old roads of eastern Lakeland*, Westmorland Gazette, Kendal.

Whaley D, *A dictionary of Lake District place-names*, University of Nottingham, Nottingham, 2006.